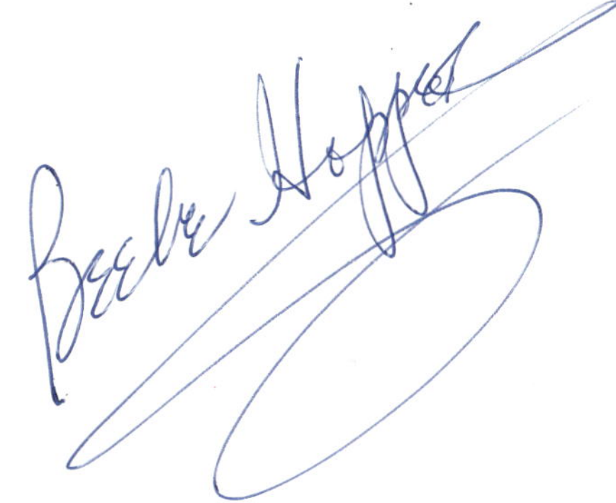

# WILDFOWL PAINTING

## *The Art of Feather Stroke Painting*

• Basic Instruction Section

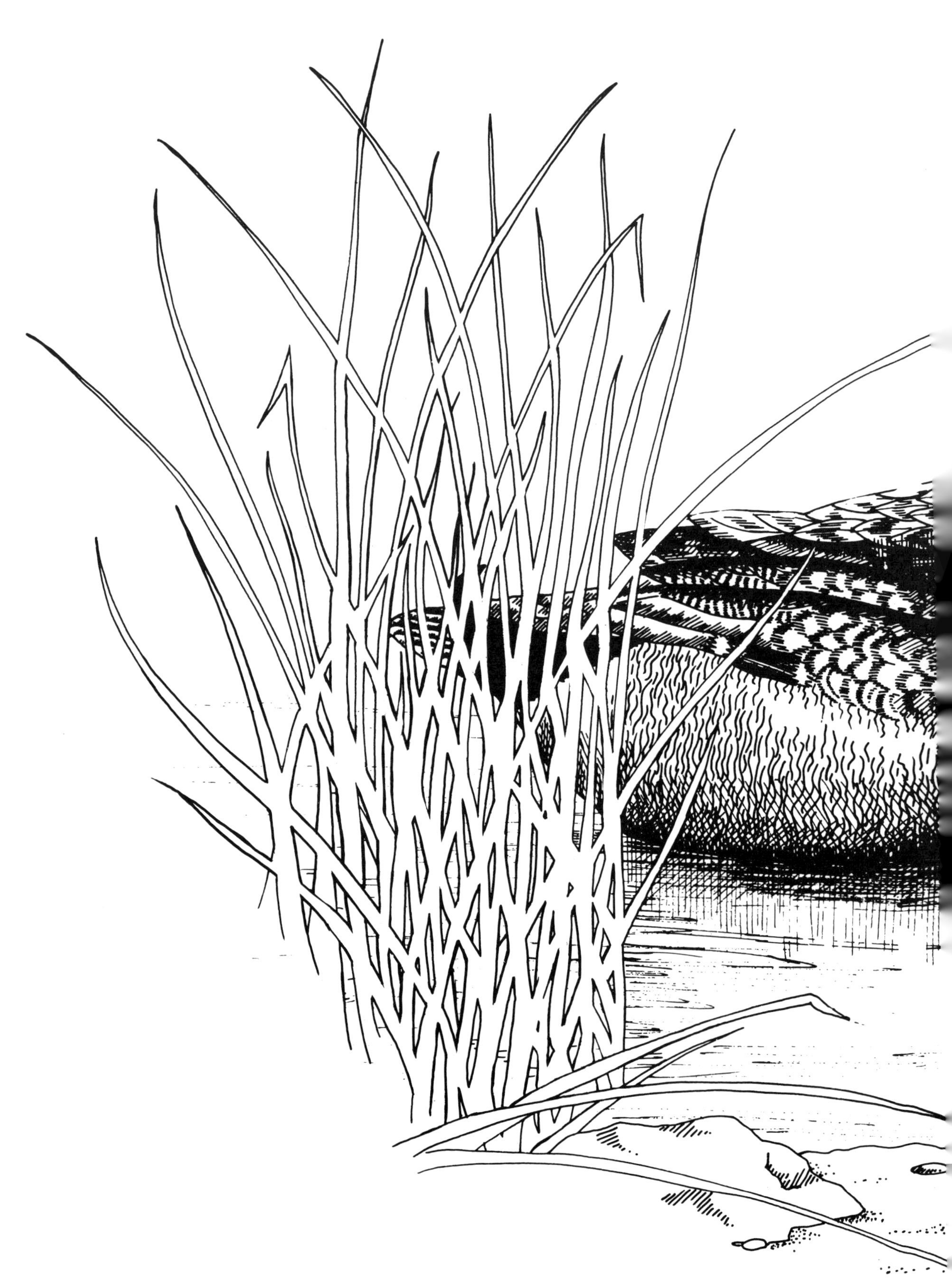

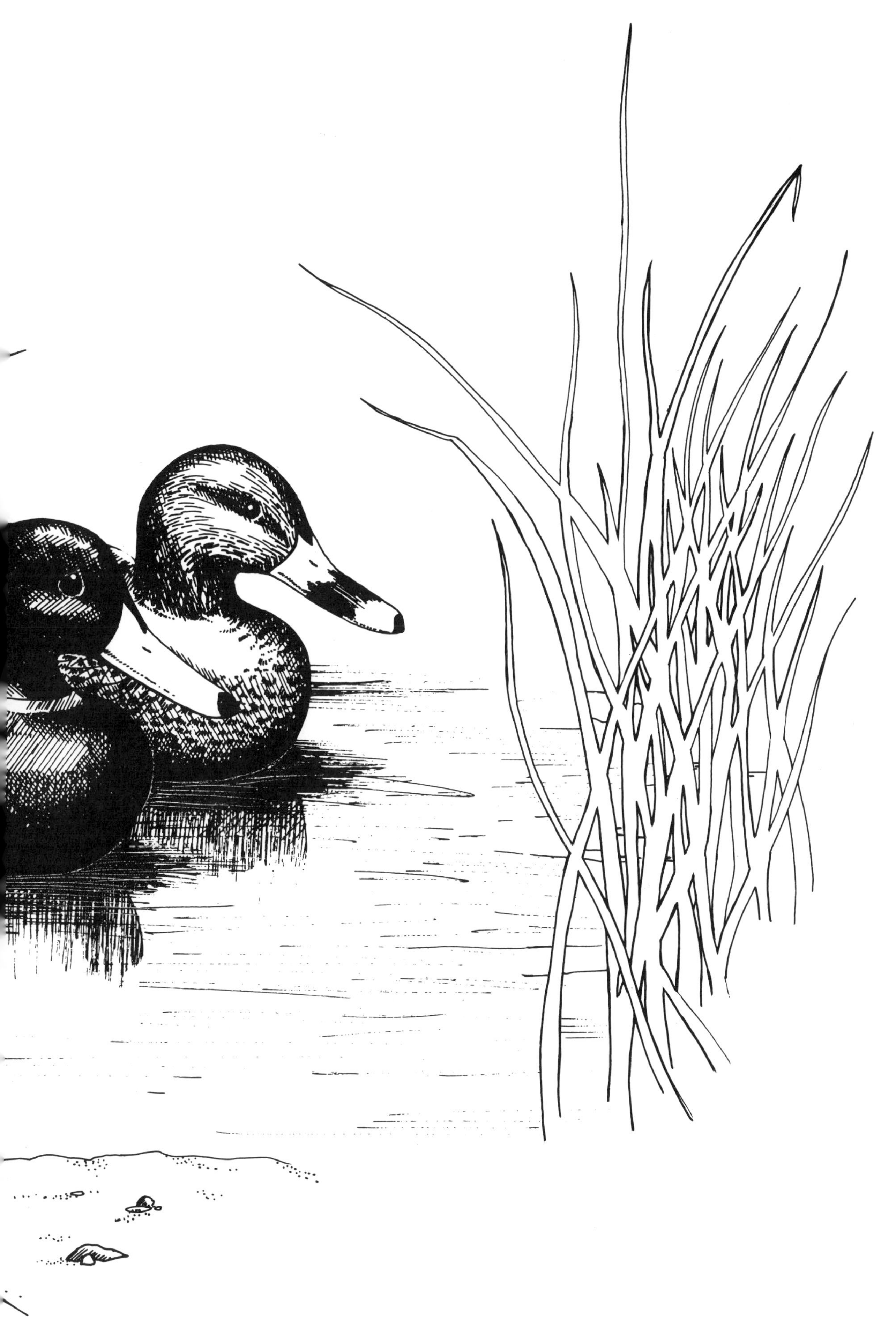

# Featured Wildfowl:

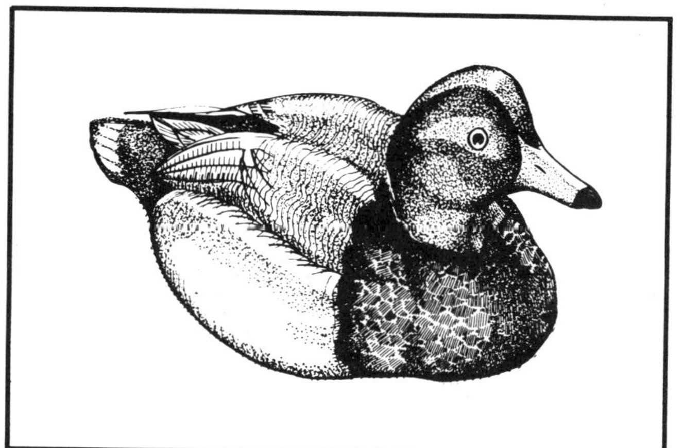

Red Head Drake

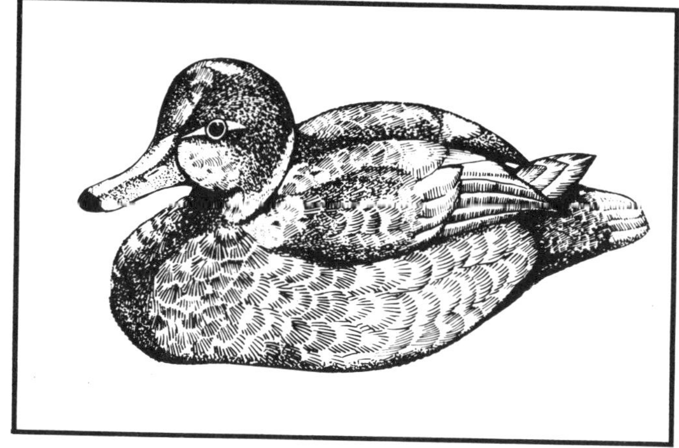

Red Head Hen

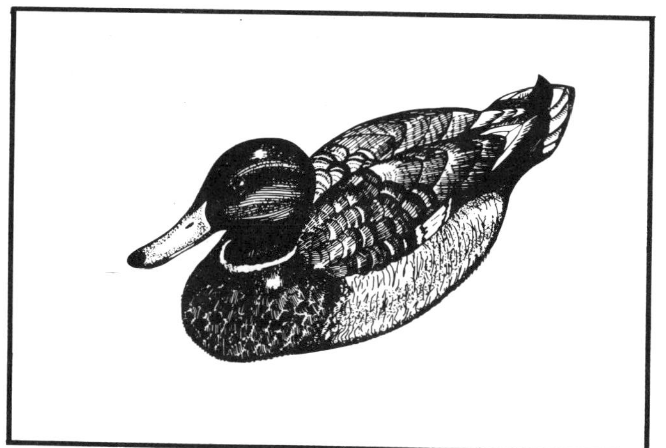

Mallard Drake

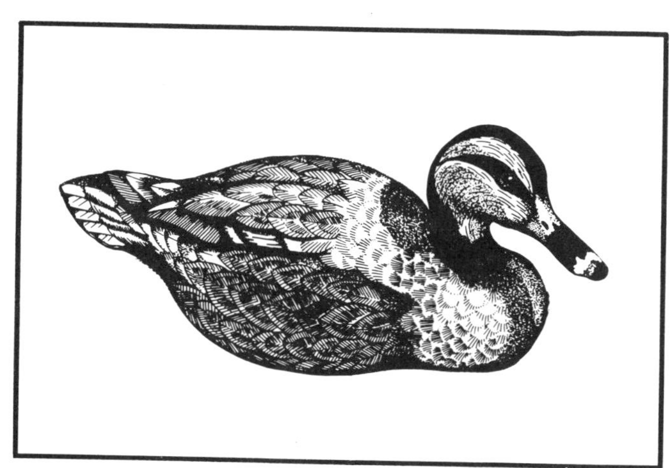

Mallard Hen

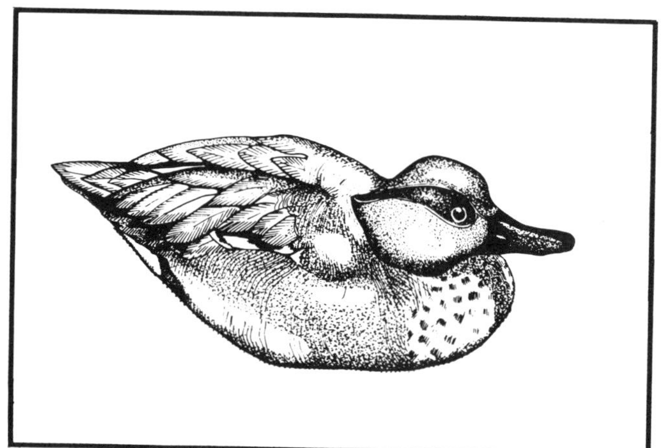

Green Winged Teal Drake

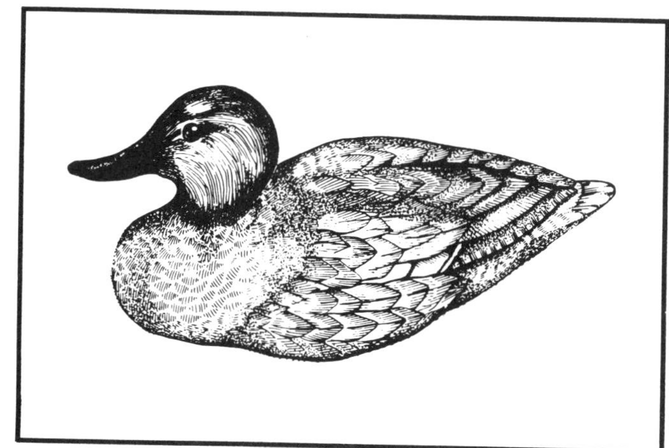

Green Winged Teal Hen

# CONTENTS

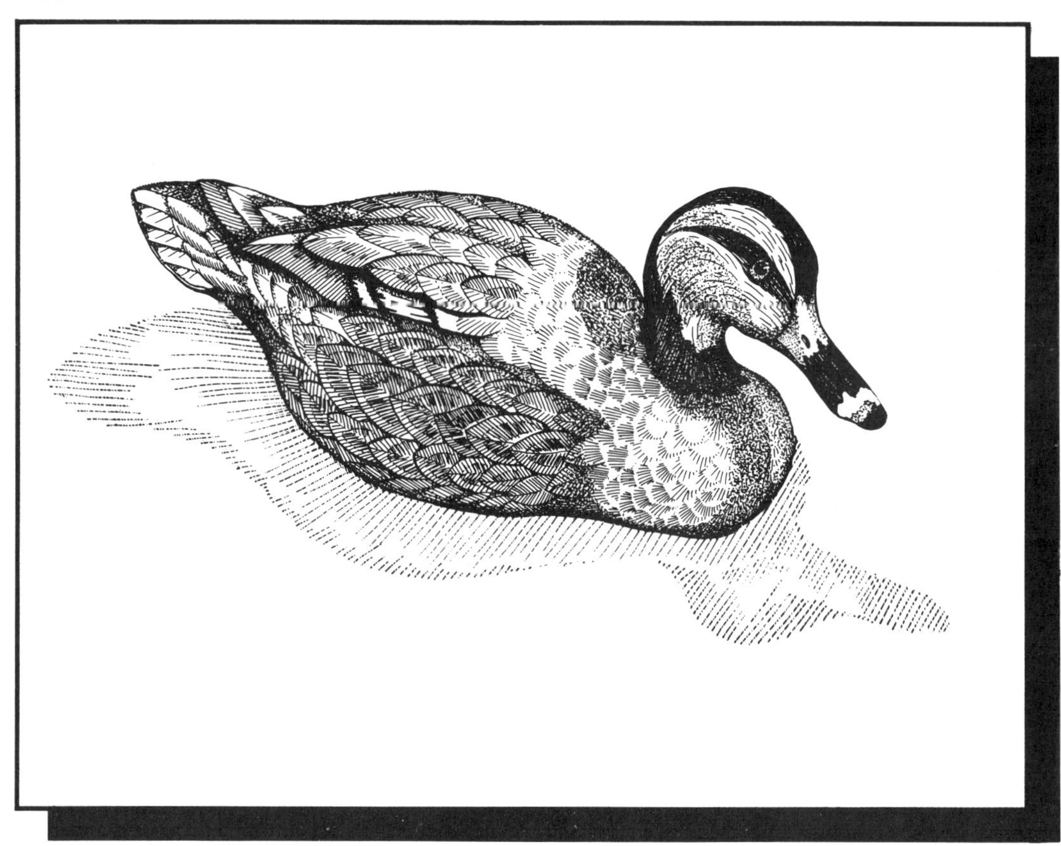

Beebe Hopper is the author of several wildfowl painting publications which can be purchased at your local art and craft supply store or write to: Beebe Hopper, 731 Beech Avenue, Chula Vista, CA 92010.

*Featherstrokes - The Basics of Painting Feathers*
*Featherstrokes for Canvasbacks*
*Featherstrokes for Mallards*

Beebe Hopper brushes are manufactured by Langnickel, Inc.. For further information on these brushes write to:

Langnickel, Inc.
229 West 28th Street
New York, New York 10001

The decoy blanks shown throughout this publication are courtesy of:

Big Sky Carvers - Bozeman, Montana
Dolington Woodcrafts - Newtown, Pennsylvania

All Permalba Acrylic colors, Permalba Gesso, matte and gloss medium, and support products can be found in your local art and craft supply store or you can write to the following address for information on where they can be obtained.

Martin/F. Weber Company
2727 Southampton Road
Philadelphia, PA 19154

# DEDICATION

*To Arvid Langnickel, the founder of Langnickel, Inc., whose distinctive brushes have provided painting pleasures to so many painters and artists.*


# ACKNOWLEDGEMENTS

*My grateful appreciation is offered to Ed Flax for having faith in me.*

*To Phillip Myer, for without his guiding hand, this project could not have been accomplished.*

# MEET THE AUTHOR

*Beebe Hopper has always been involved in one form or another of the art field. Upon moving from Mississippi to California in 1950, a whole new world of creative endeavors opened up; ceramics, china painting, and crafts of all kinds were introduced to her. Jim, her husband, encouraged her to begin oil painting. Additionally, about 20 years ago, she began classes in the adult education system of San Diego County. She fell in love with the arts and since has been devoted full time to the art field. Watercolor painting, intaglio etching, and acrylic painting of bird carvings are all parts of her creativity today.*

*She studied at the California College of Arts and Crafts, Oakland, California as well as with such leading artists as Zoltan Szabo, Bennett Bradbury, Bill DeShazo and Bob Landry.*

*Her work is displayed in the Wildlife Art Museum, Salisbury, Maryland. She is a regularly invited participant for exhibits across the nation including The Waterfowl Festival, Easton, Maryland; The Ward Foundation Carving and Art Show, Salisbury, Maryland; and Pacific Southwest Wildfowl Arts, San Diego, California. Beebe is a consultant to and travels for brush manufacturer, Langnickel, Inc. of New York City and for art material manufacturer and book publisher, Martin/F. Weber Company, Philadelphia, Pennsylvania, demonstrating a simple, easy technique for painting bird carvings in a realistic manner. She conducts seminars in this technique on a nationwide basis.*

*Beebe's lifelong interest in nature led to the specialization in painting wildfowl and related subjects. Professional organizations with which she is affiliated include the National Wildlife Federation, Audubon Society, Ducks Unlimited, and Pacific Southwest Wildfowl Arts. Beebe is a member of the National Advisory Board of the Ward Foundation, Salisbury, Maryland.*

*She has published three booklets on how to paint feathers. "Featherstrokes - The Basics of Painting Feathers", "Featherstrokes for Canvasbacks" and "Featherstrokes for Mallards" are excellent foundation booklets on wildfowl painting.*

*For thirty-five years, she has been married to Jim Hopper, Commander U.S. Navy (retired). Upon his retirement from the Navy he devoted his time to carving birds, most of which Beebe paints. The Hopper's have a married daughter, Holly and two grandchildren.*

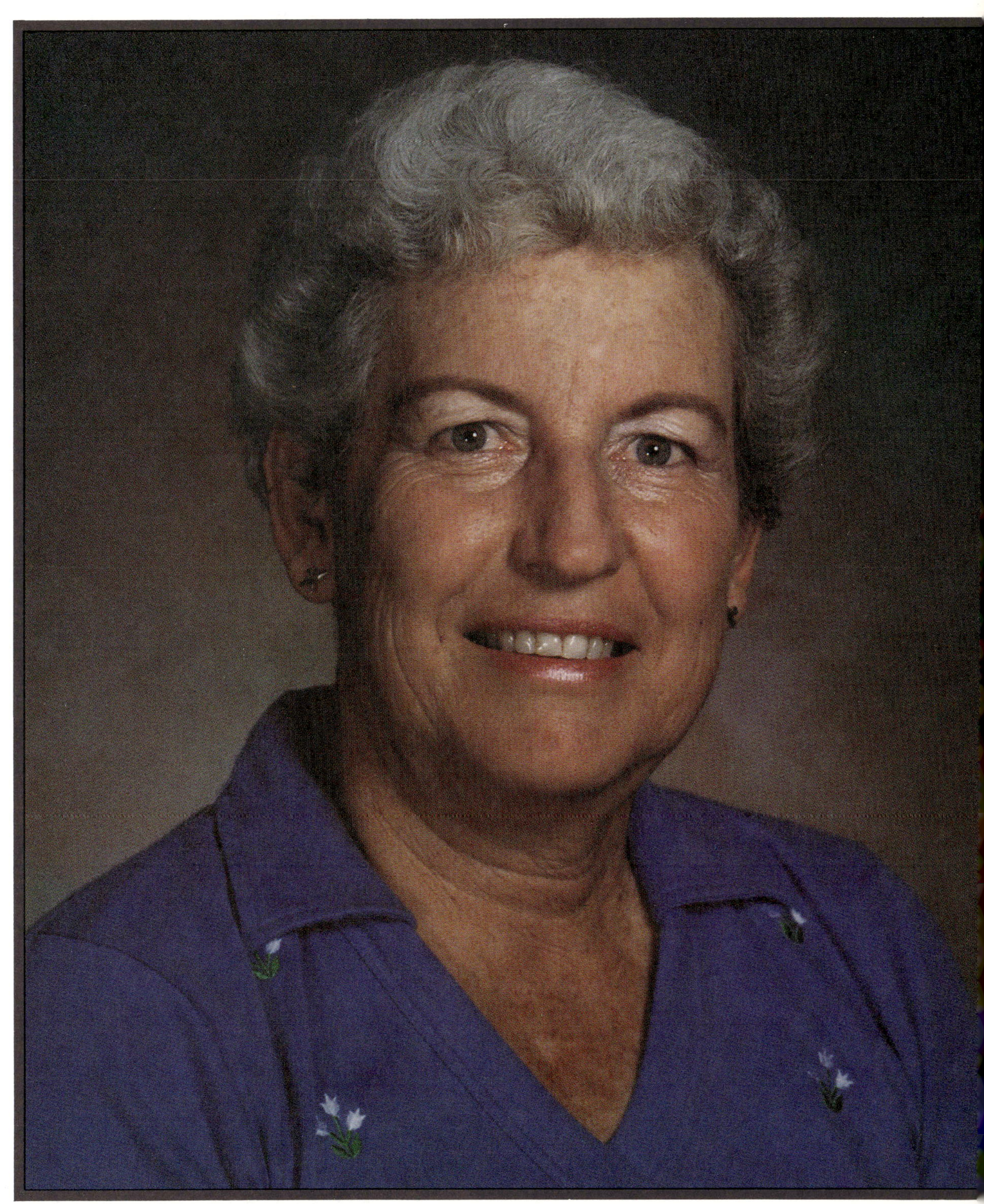

Photography by Bruce Pitcher

# INTRODUCTION

*There is an easy way to paint realistic feathers for wildfowl painting! That is what this book is all about. A technique is presented which is so simple that anyone who knows how a feather looks can quickly master rendering wildfowl effects.*

*A feather is a feather is a feather! Whether it is on a duck, goose, songbird, shorebird, hummingbird, chicken, bird-of-paradise or whatever the variety may be. The feather painting techniques that are taught in this book are just one approach. They are simple, easy style methods which provide the beginner with the background for successful ventures from the start. Techniques are used on textured carvings, carvings with the feather pattern burned in, or on smooth surfaces. The techniques can be used with any media: oils, acrylics, or watercolor. The only difference will occur in the consistency of the paint. Acrylics are the simplest media for the beginner learning these methods. Acrylics hold the bristles of the brush in the desired positions for different shapes and sizes of feather effects. You must work harder at learning and achieving the right consistency for the oil or watercolor medias. Consistency of media is a technique which comes from practice and experimenting. It is a feel of the brush and paint to your fingertips. When you begin to paint and mix with your media, you will learn the feel of paint consistencies.*

*Do not be afraid to begin! Remember, it is not yet a great work of art, it is only a piece of wood, canvas, or paper! You can repaint it as many times as you choose. Putting this thought into perspective gives you psychological freedom to begin to create. So why are you waiting?*

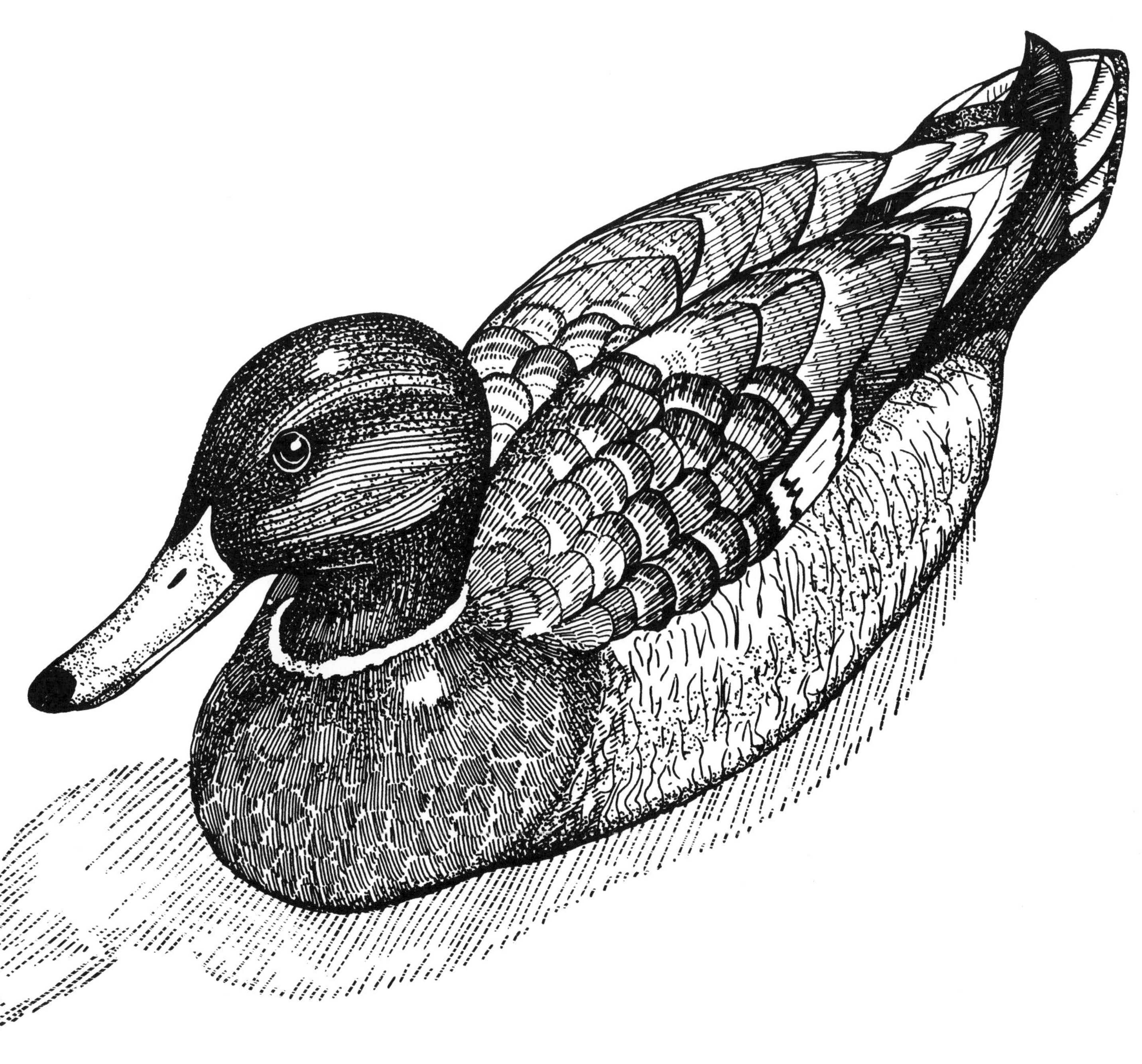

# SUPPLIES

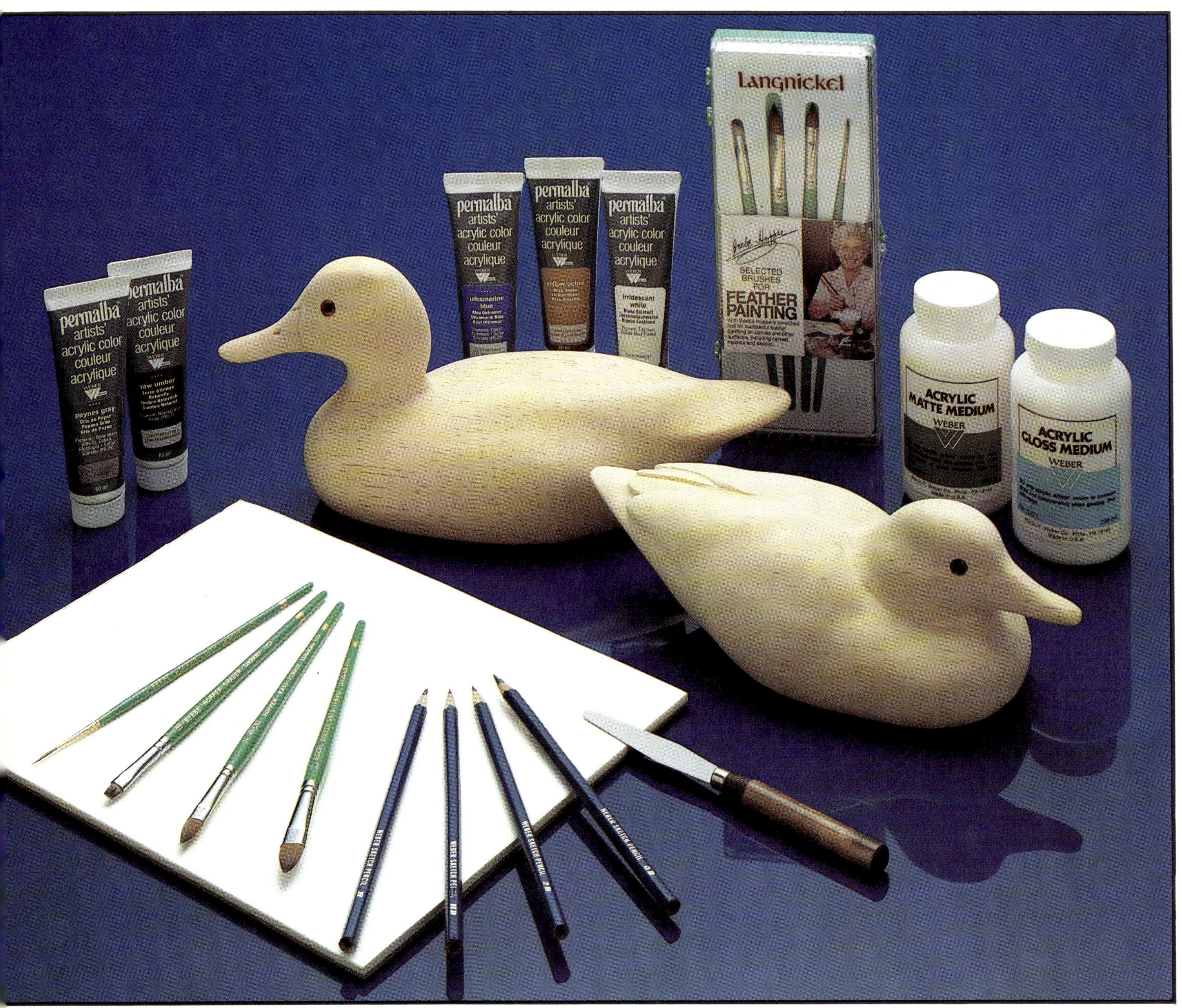


*Basic supplies used in painting of wildfowl art.*

Supplies used throughout this book are listed below.

***Matte medium*** - Used in conjunction with the vermiculation technique and for applying a finish coat on the completed wildfowl carvings and paintings.

***Palette*** - A piece of glass with white cardboard or paper underneath is best. It provides a firm surface for fanning the Kats Tongue brush. However, the waxed coated disposable palette is very convenient.

***Paper towels*** - Several folded thicknesses of paper towels will be needed for blotting of excess water and paint from your brushes.

***Painting knife*** - A flat blade knife will be needed to mix your colors.

***Fine grade sandpaper*** - For smoothing rough areas of carved wildfowl.

***Exacto knife*** - For cleaning paint off the glass eyes of carved wildfowl.

***Water container*** - A plastic or glass jar or brush basin for cleaning your brushes.

***Pencil*** - HB or 2B pencil for drawing or sketching the designs on the surfaces.

**Permalba Acrylic Colors**

***Titanium White*** - A pure white, used alone for highlights or mixed with colors to create tints or hues.

***Unbleached Titanium*** - An off-white used with almost any color, especially Raw Umber to create the many shades needed to paint feathers.

***Raw Umber*** - A dark grayish brown, the most important color in painting most birds. Please note, there is a vast difference in the Raw Umber color made from different manufacturers of artist's colors. Permalba Raw Umber has been formulated to properly match the color native to so many birds, whether it is used as a single coat or as a layered wash of color.

***Burnt Umber*** - A rich dark earth tone brown used throughout wildfowl painting.

***Ivory Black*** - A black which is warmer and more transparent than other blacks. A color used to tint other hues and for the application of the darks.

***Burnt Sienna*** - A reddish brown which is a very warm earth tone applied throughout the painting process.

***Bright Red*** - A rich intense red mixed with other hues to create accent areas and some of the bright areas of the species.

***Paynes Gray*** - A cool steel gray applied in the body and bill sections of many of the wildfowl species.

***Hookers Green*** - A dark transparent forest green used in the application of the head of the mallard drake.

***Phthalo Green*** - A middle value green.

***Ultramarine Blue*** - An intense bright blue used in the speculum of some wildfowl species.

***Yellow Ochre*** - A light natural earth tone used throughout wildfowl painting.

***Cadmium Orange*** - A bright mid-value orange used in mixtures for color area such as the bills.

***Dioxazine Purple*** - A deep intense purple hue used for the speculum area in some wildfowl species.

***Cadmium Yellow Medium*** - A rich bright middle value yellow for application in color mixtures. A color not typically used alone in wildfowl painting.

***Iridescent Gold*** - A sparkling, dazzling gold used in feather stroke painting and color mixtures.

***Iridescent Green*** - A deep green with sparkling effects used in some head areas of the wildfowl species.

***Iridescent Blue*** - A dazzling blue for application in the speculum area of the wildfowl species.

***Iridescent Purple*** - A deep purple with a rainbowlike glow used in select areas of wildfowl painting.

***Iridescent White*** - A pure white hue with a sparkling glitterlike effect, which can be added to a standard color to give iridescence.

# MATERIALS

IMPORTANT!! The quality of your work is in direct relationship to the quality of the materials that you use in completing that work. Remember, your materials are your tools. A good tool works for you, a poor tool works against you. So, it is advised to have the very best brushes and paints available. This also includes carving blanks, canvas, watercolor paper, and so on.

**Media**

For *painting in the round*, (carvings and sculpture) I prefer to use the acrylics. One advantage is the quick drying time, which enables you to finish an item without a long delay. When working with oil color, drying time is slow. A special hint is the use of a hair dryer which speeds the drying process immeasurably. Blending acrylics is easy if the working areas are kept damp.

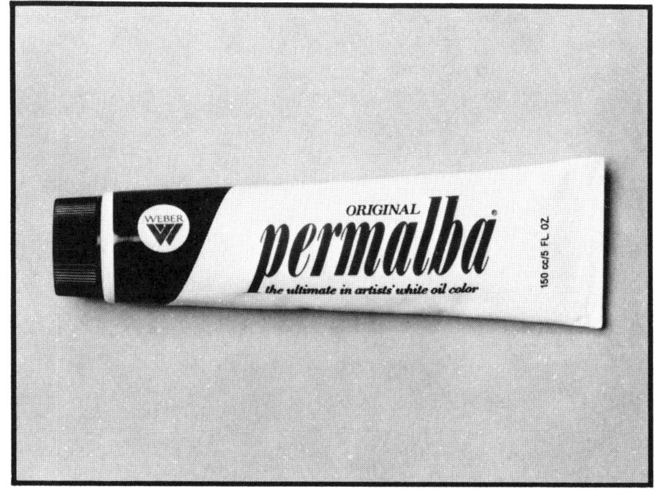


*Artists' oil colors are used in canvas painting.*

Permalba acrylics, manufactured by Martin/F. Weber Company, Philadelphia, Pennsylvania are paints of superb quality, both in texture and brilliance of hue. The flowing quality from the brush to the surface is excellent.

Canvas painting in oils, I feel, is a very exciting medium! They are a media which enables easy repair of mistakes. Permalba oils have been my personal choice for years. The consistency of the paint, the blending of the colors, and the vibrance of color cannot be surpassed. Permalba oils are a real joy to use.

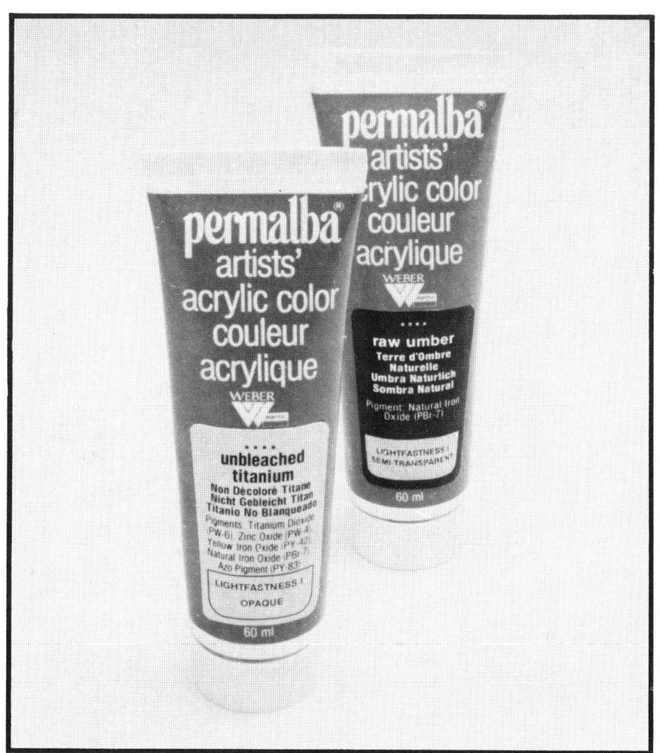


*Quality artists' acrylic colors are the choosen media.*

**Brushes**

One cannot stress the value of good brushes enough. Many years ago an artist from Palm Springs, California, introduced me to Langnickel brushes and it has been a love affair for me ever since. One can pay more for a brush, but one cannot buy a better quality brush than a Langnickel. The Beebe Hopper Feather Painting Brushes are manufactured by Langnickel, Incorporated. The Beebe Hopper Kats Tongue has been a mainstay for me when working in oils. When I began painting dimensional carved wildfowl, the brushes adapted so well to feather painting I felt that Mr. Langnickel must have designed them for just that purpose. The Beebe Hopper Shader is ideal for canvas painting, especially for laying in backgrounds. The students and fellow artists I have introduced this brush to, feel they do not want to be without it at anytime. When this brush is used as a shader for wildfowl feather painting, the results, without a doubt, are unmatchable. The Beebe Hopper Liner works well with all three media-oil, watercolor, or acrylic. The bristles are long enough to give the freedom of a rigger brush but short enough for control of detail work.

# BRUSH FACTS

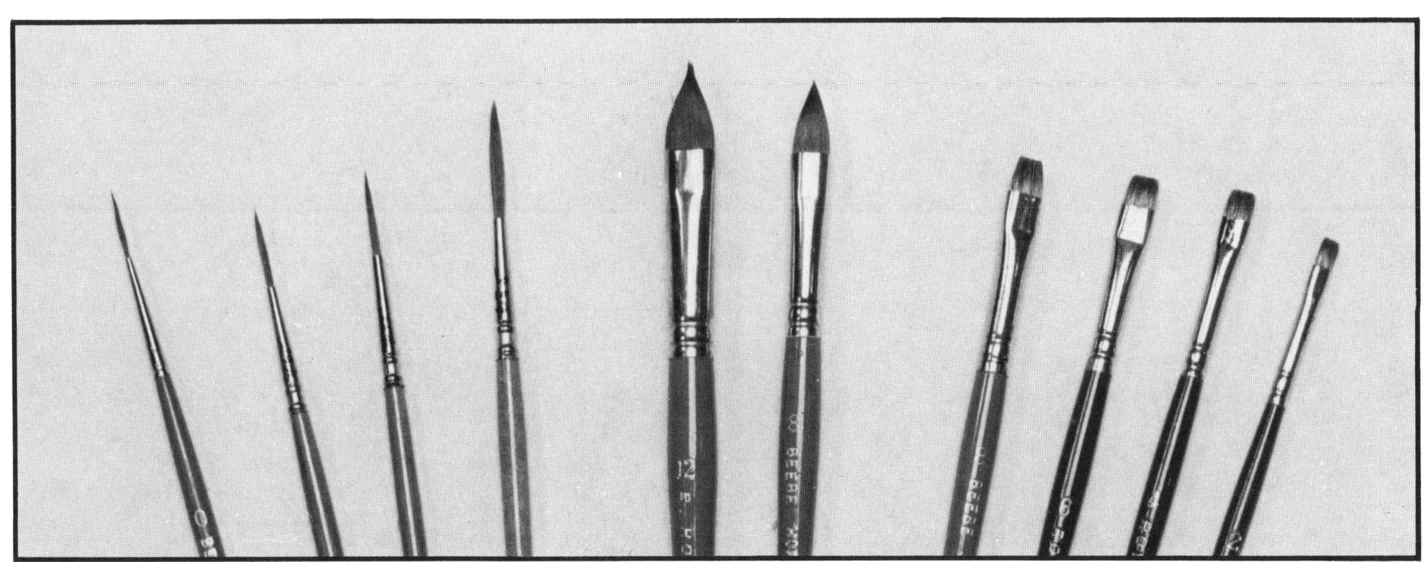

***Brushes***
*An assortment of varying brush styles will be needed to create the different wildfowl painting techniques taught in this book.*

There are three basic elements to each brush; the hair, the metal ferrule and the wooden handle.

The hair selected for the head of the brush, animal or synthetic, is the most important element. It must have resiliency, durability, and the quality to keep a point or hold a sharp edge.

Brush hair falls into two categories—soft and stiff. Stiff bristles are usually hog or nylon. Soft hairs generally used are kolinsky, weasel, ox, sabeline, squirrel, pony, and goat. The *red sable* as known to artists, comes from different species of the squirrel, weasel, or rodent family which live in cold climates, not from the sable animal.

Various brush raw materials are listed below with a short description of each. Please familiarize yourself with these different types, to enable you to distinguish the quality levels of brushes when purchasing them.

***Kolinsky*** - known as *Finest Red Sable*, this hair, possessing exceptional spring and fine pointing quality, comes from the kolinsky animal which is native to Northern China, Southern Russia, and Siberia. Only the hairs from the tail of the animal are used.

***Weasel*** - known as *Fine or Good Quality* red sable, these hairs come from the tails of the weasel family of animals.

***Squirrel*** - a very soft hair taken from tails of different species of squirrel. Painting quality is excellent.

***Goat*** - A soft hair used in lesser quality or cosmetic brushes.

***Pony*** - from the mane and body of ponies.

***Hog*** - the bristles of the spinal section of wild boars from Northern China are used for the top of the line white bristle brushes.

***Nylon*** - a man made synthetic product used alone or blended with various natural hairs for all styles of brushes. Quality varies a great deal -until recently synthetic brushes were not produced at a very high quality level. Today there are some quality synthetic brushes being produced.

***Handles*** - The wooden handles are made from hardwood in either short or long length. Wooden handles are usually coated with a sturdy lacquer paint coating. Plastic handles are generally used for brushes with nylon bristles.

***Ferrules*** - Nickel plated brass or aluminum is used. Most ferrules are seamless to prevent splitting.

***Ox*** - taken from oxen native to Central Europe and North and South America.

***Sabeline*** - a medium grade hair used for watercolor, lettering and stroke work. Made from dyed ox hair.

# TECHNIQUES AND BASICS

**Preparation**

To begin to paint a dimensional wildfowl decoy, you must start with a well sanded and primed carved decoy. First, apply a wood sealer to the entire decoy. Let dry. After the carved decoy is sealed, apply a white base primer coat. This can be an acrylic, latex paint, or gesso product. Let coat dry. Now sand the prime coat smooth with fine grade sandpaper.

**Brush Information**

*Feather strokes with the Beebe Hopper Kats Tongue brush* - The Beebe Hopper Kats Tongue brush is simple and ideal to use for painting the individual feathers of the wildfowl. A large size Kats Tongue brush will create large feathers and will also taper down to create very small feathers. On the other hand, a small size brush will not make feathers larger than its maximum width when fanned out. The Beebe Hopper Kats Tongue brush #12 is used almost exclusively.

This particular brush will need to be "trained" to hold the proper form. To train this brush, remember to use it in the same direction each time. This is easy to remember if you use it with the writing on the handle facing away from you. Work the brush into the paint and water thoroughly. Fan the brush by pressing down firmly all the way to the ferrule. Twist carefully back and forth and the brush will form a fan shape. Refer to Photo #1. Slowly draw the brush back and up in the same motion. This is an important stroke motion to learn. Refer to Photo #2. This action will form an arc of the bristles. The brush is now ready to paint feather strokes. You must remember a light touch is necessary when painting feathers. To paint feathers, hold the brush almost upright and using a flick of the fingers, lightly stroke the bristles toward yourself. Refer to Photo #3 and Illustration #1.

For creating a medium sized feather, reduce the arc of the fanned brush by rolling the sides of the brush inward. Refer to Photo #4 and Illustration #2. For smaller feathers, reduce the arc again. Refer to Photo #5 and Illustration #3. To paint tiny feathers for the head and neck areas of the duck decoys, press the sides of the arc together with your fingers to form a "tent" or inverted "V". Refer to Photo #6 and Illustration #4. Hold the brush perpendicular to the surface and with a light touch paint the tiny

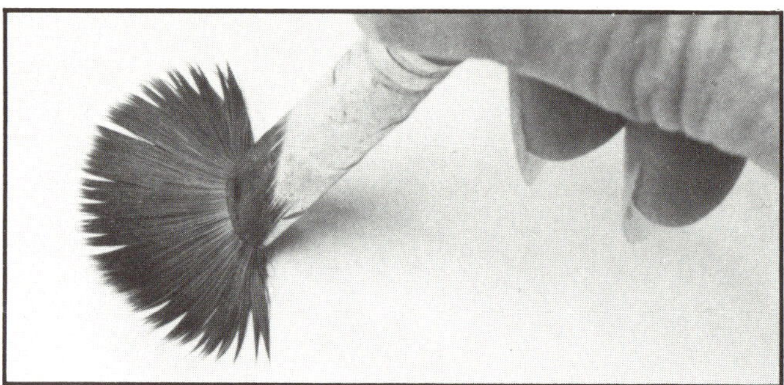

***Photo #1***
*The brush is fanned to its maximum width by twisting the brush back and forth.*

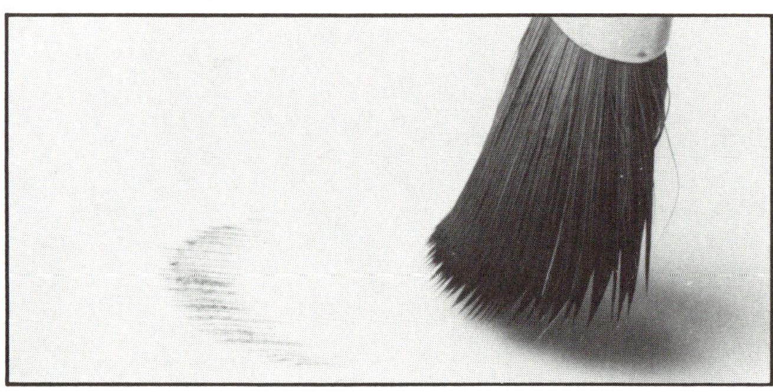

***Photo #2***
*After the brush has been fanned to its maximum potential, release pressure and slowly draw the brush back and up in the same motion.*

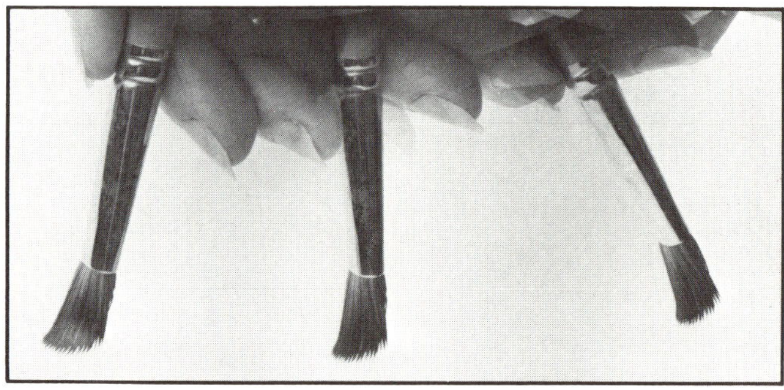

***Photo #3***
*The feather stroke motion is shown above by flicking the bristles of the brush toward yourself.*

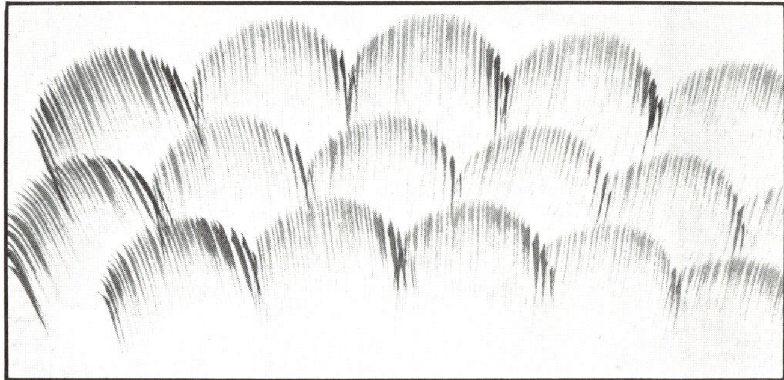

***Illustration #1***
*The following feather strokes were completed with the Beebe Hopper Kats Tongue brush #12 fanned to its maximum potential.*

feathers. If bristles split or separate, use more paint but only enough to hold the bristles in the desired position.

*Vermiculation with the Beebe Hopper Kats Tongue brush* - The dictionary defines vermiculation as "to ornate with winding and waving lines like the track of a worm." In wildfowl painting, vermiculation techniques create feathers which have a multitude of fine, wavy or crooked lines. To accomplish this, flatten the arc of the Beebe Hopper Kats Tongue brush into a shallow curve or straight line. Use a light touch with stipple-like motion. For more specific information, see detailed section on vermiculation. You may add a pattern into the vermiculation by separating the bristles into small sections by using something thin, such as your fingernail.

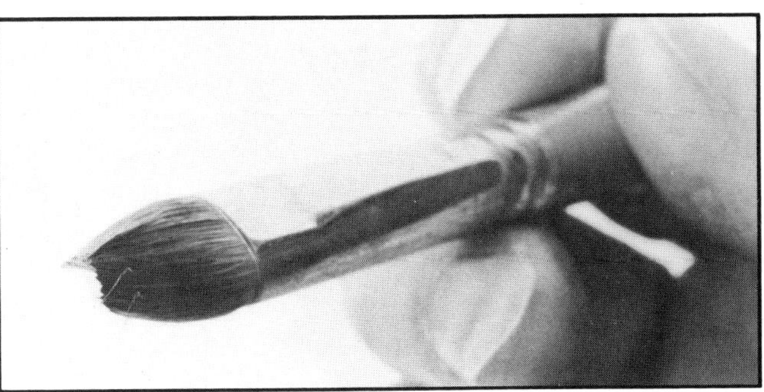

***Photo #5***
*The arc of the brush is reduced again by rolling the sides of the brush.*

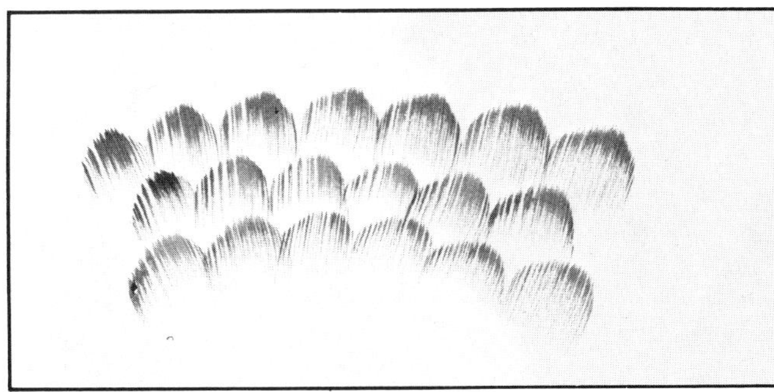

***Illustration #3***
*These feather strokes were completed using the Kats Tongue brush #12 rolled to a small size.*

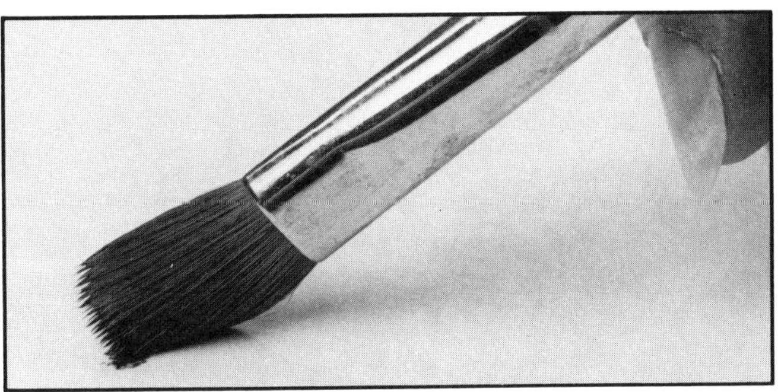

***Photo #4***
*To create medium size feathers, reduce the arc of the fanned brush by rolling the sides of the brush inward.*

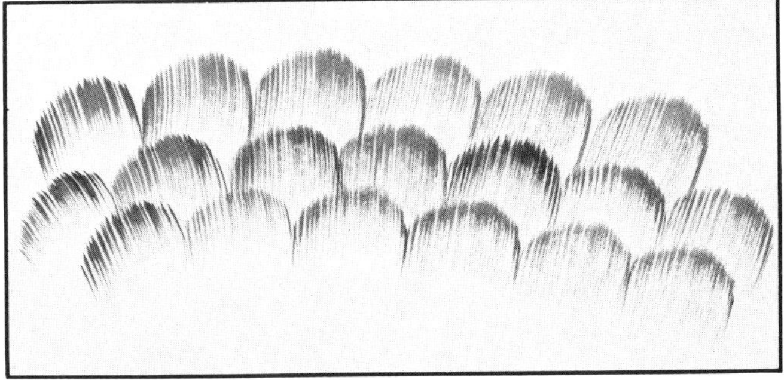

***Illustration #2***
*The above feather strokes were completed with the Beebe Hopper Kats Tongue brush #12 rolled inward to a medium size.*

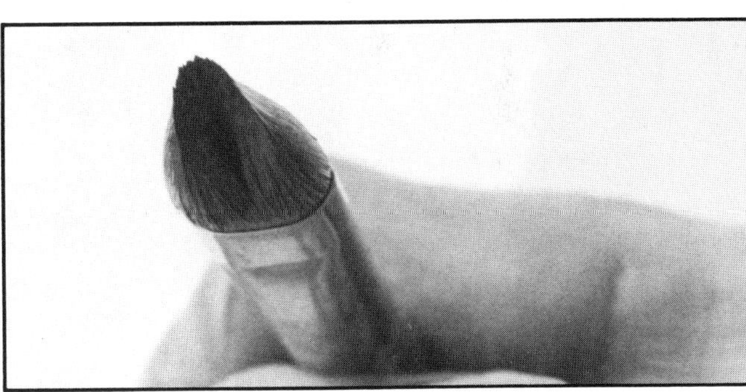

***Photo #6***
*To create the smallest feather stroke with the #12 brush, make a "tent" or inverted "V" out of the brush tip.*

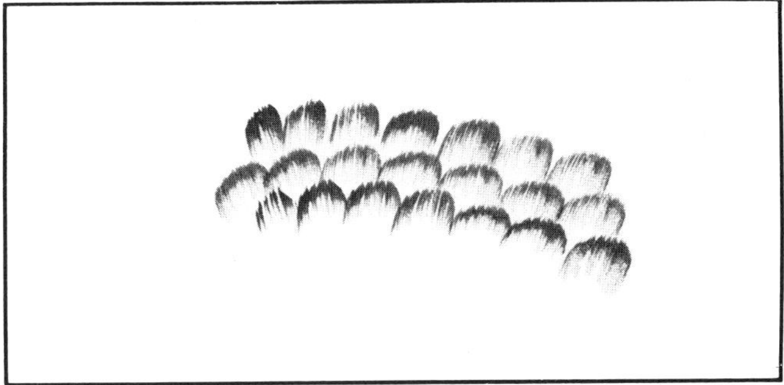

***Illustration #4***
*Feather strokes created with the #12 brush with "tent" or inverted "V" shape.*

# TECHNIQUES AND BASICS

**Linework**

The Beebe Hopper Liner Brush is used for fine line detail on carvings, and also makes great grass and twiggy trees in landscape painting. To complete linework techniques, the paint should be the consistency of ink. Saturate the brush with thin paint, brace your hand and use only the *tip of the brush.* Refer to Photo #7 and Illustration #5. It works like a fountain pen. The paint keeps flowing down to the tip. When lifting off the palette, roll the brush and lift to form a sharp point.

**Shading**

The Beebe Hopper Shader Brush is ideal for canvas painting, especially for applying foundations in backgrounds. The students I have introduced this brush to feel they cannot paint without it. The bristles come to a fine razor edge and is used for shading on the elongated feathers of many birds. Refer to Photo #8 and Illustration #6.

**Washes**

A wash simply means a small amount of paint mixed into a larger amount of water. There are thin washes, medium washes, and heavy washes. It is difficult to define exact amounts. A "rule of thumb" for a thin wash is one drop of paint to thirty drops of water; for a medium wash it would be more paint and less water, and for a heavy wash it would be even more paint and less water. Refer to Illustration #7.

**Finishing**

One way to finish a carving is by applying a generous coat of matte medium over the completed bird. This gives a satin finish, neither dull nor glossy. The matte medium looks very

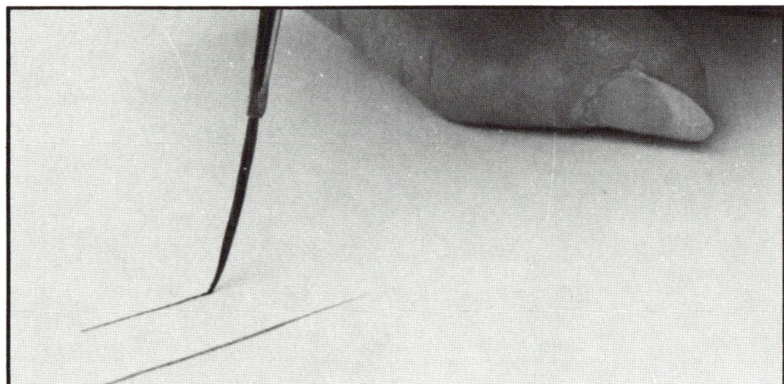

***Photo #7***
*Use only the tip of the Liner brush to paint the linework and detail areas.*

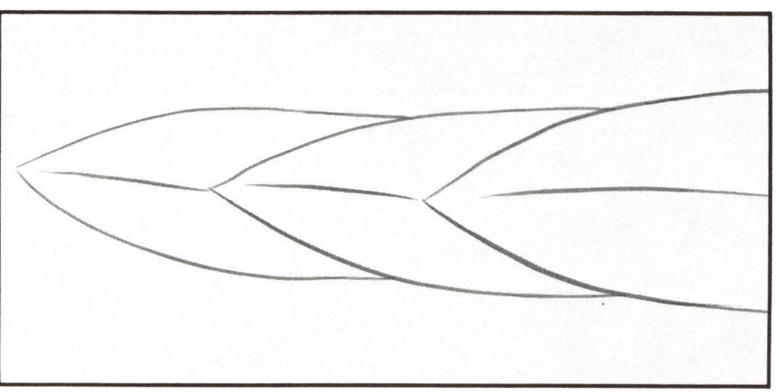

***Illustration #5***
*Linework created to outline the feathers using a Beebe Hopper Liner brush #0.*

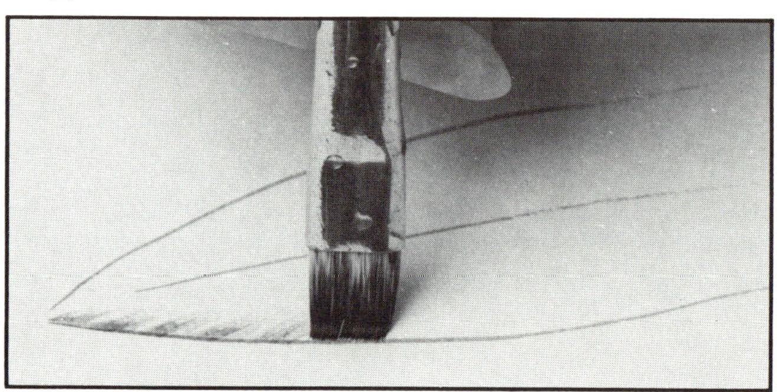

***Photo #8***
*Shading the elongated feathers of the wildfowl is accomplished by stroking from the edge of the feather toward the center.*

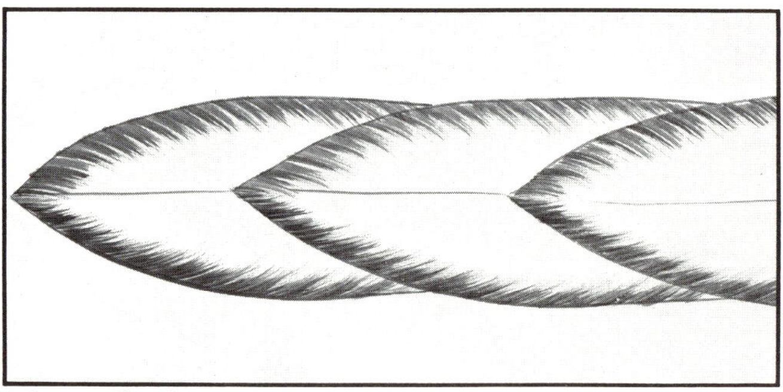

***Illustration #6***
*Elongated feathers shaded at edge with a Beebe Hopper Shader brush #10.*

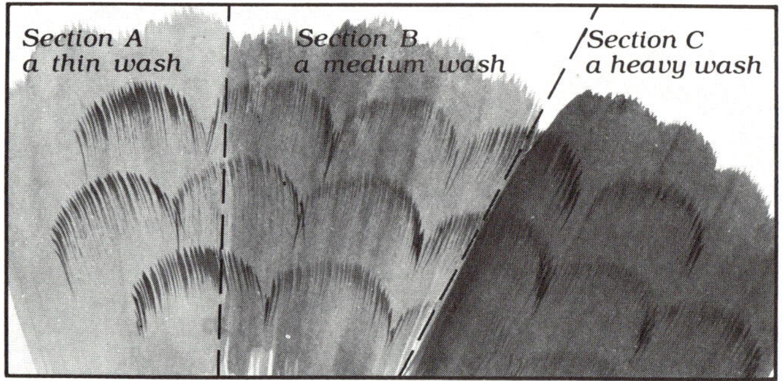


***Illustration #7***
*Applying washes at varying degrees of opacity can be accomplished by changing the amount of pigment and water.*

milky upon application but when dry, becomes transparent. Apply the matte medium in a very even application with a soft hair varnish brush or sponge brush.

### Vermiculation

#### *Matte Medium Method*

Mix a small amount of black paint into acrylic matte medium to desired shade of gray for a particular species of bird. This mix will dry with a hard edge very quickly so *work in small areas* at a time. First, brush clear matte medium around the edge of a small working area to keep a hard edge from forming. Refer to Illustration #8. Freely brush on the gray mix in a thick coat working into half the width of the clear medium around the edge. Work quickly, stipple (arched or straight into the mixture) with Beebe Hopper Kats Tongue brush #12. Refer to Illustration #9. The Beebe Hopper Shader brush in desired size may also be used to complete this technique. Refer to Illustration #10.

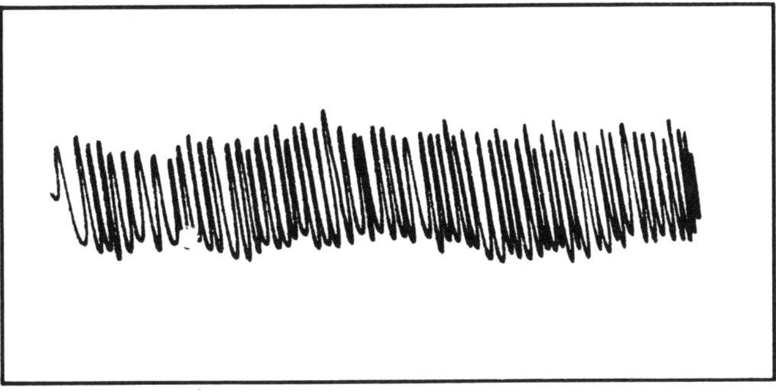

***Illustration #8***
*Place clear matte medium on edge of area where vermiculation technique will be placed. Stroke one half of the brush loaded with the gray mixture into this area to prevent hard edges from forming.*

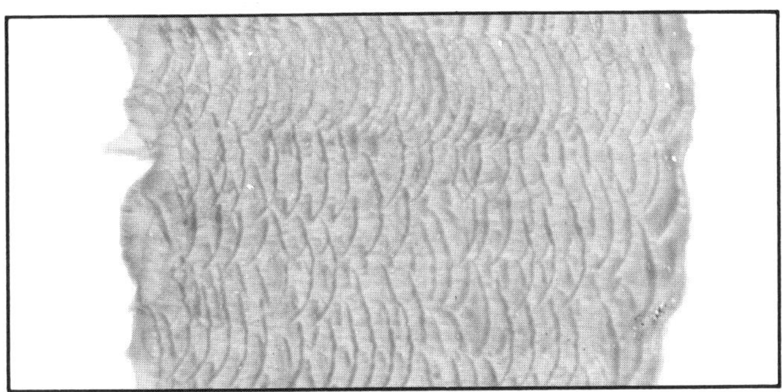

***Illustration #9***
*Vermiculation technique in an arched pattern created with matte medium method using the Beebe Hopper Kats Tongue brush #12.*

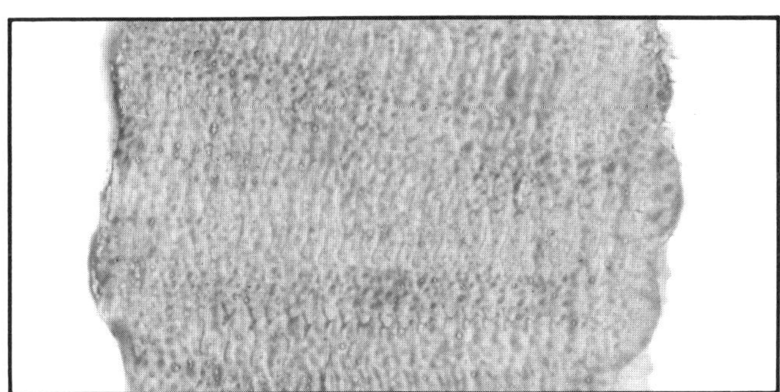

***Illustration #10***
*Vermiculation technique in a straight pattern created with matte medium method using the Beebe Hopper Shader brush #18.*

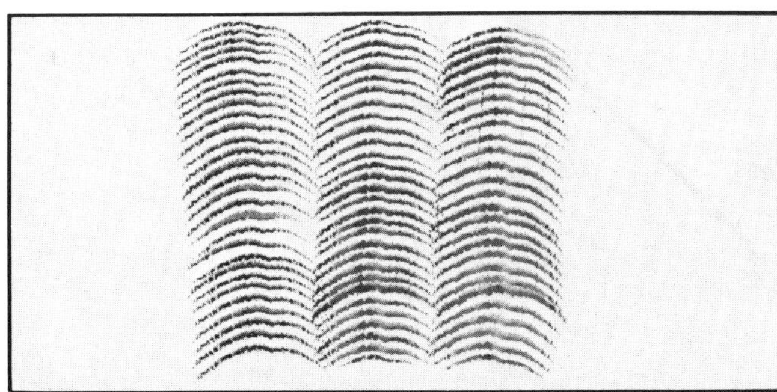

***Illustration #11***
*Vermiculation technique in an arched pattern created with the brush method using the Beebe Hopper Kats Tongue brush #12 fanned to the maximum size.*

#### Brush Method

For arched pattern, use the Beebe Hopper Kats Tongue brush fanned to the desired size. Refer to Illustration #11 and #12. For a straight pattern, use the Beebe Hopper Shader brush in desired size. Refer to Illustration #13. Paint should be a fairly thin consistency and the brush should be filled with paint. Apply the stipple stroke technique with light touch.

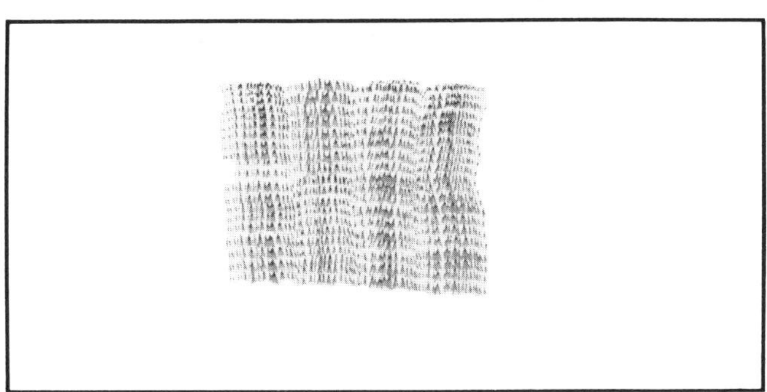

***Illustration #12***
*Vermiculation technique in a straight pattern created with the brush method using the Beebe Hopper Kats Tongue brush #12.*

### Liner Brush Method

For this technique, paint should be mixed to a thin consistency. Using the tip of Beebe Hopper Liner brush, paint fine, wavy lines varying the directions slightly so the lines will not be perfectly parallel. Refer to Illustration # 14. Or, using the tip of the Liner brush, make tiny strokes in wavy lines. Refer to Illustration #15. The Liner brush method is much more time consuming than the previous methods discussed.

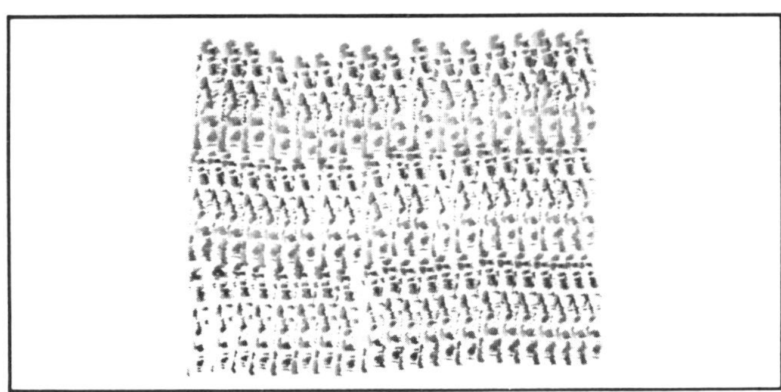

***Illustration #13***
*Vermiculation technique in a straight pattern created with the brush method using the Beebe Hopper Shader brush #18.*

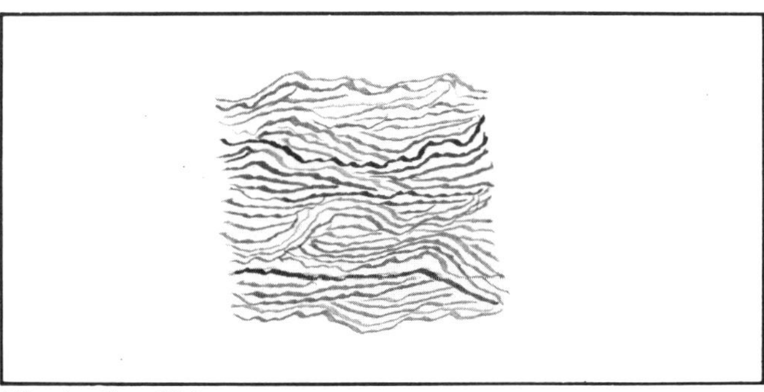

***Illustration #14***
*Vermiculation technique in a linear pattern created with the brush method using the Beebe Hopper Liner brush #0.*

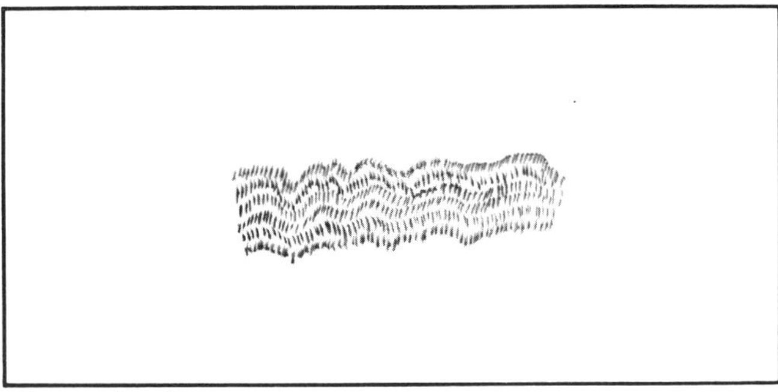

***Illustration #15***
*Vermiculation technique in a wavy line pattern created with the brush method using the Beebe Hopper Liner brush #0.*

## GLOSSARY OF BIRD DEFINITIONS

***Barbs*** - The part of the feather attached to the quill.

***Breast*** - Front chest area of the bird.

***Coverts*** - Feathers at the base of the upper tail, also at base of underneath tail area.

***Crest*** - Long feathers at the back of the head and neck.

***Crown*** - Forehead and top of the bird's head.

***Diving duck*** - Species that dives into the water for food. In order to fly from water, it must take off by running across the water. The legs of a diving duck are further back on the body than a puddle duck.

***Drake*** - A male duck.

***Eye trough*** - A recessed area in the front and back of the eye.

***Hen*** - A female duck.

***Iridescence*** - Shimmering metallic colors on feathers.

***Jowl*** - Jutting part of the jaw.

***Nail*** - The hardened area at the end of the bill.

***Neck ring*** - A narrow band of colored feathers around the throat.

***Primaries*** - The ten largest flight feathers of the wing.

***Puddle duck*** - A species that feeds in shallow water usually by tipping the head into the water while the tail is up in the air. To fly off water they spring upward. Their legs are toward the center of the body.

***Secondaries*** - The ten smaller feathers of the inner wing (Speculum).

***Sidepocket*** - Recessed area between side and back of duck.

***Speculum*** - The brilliant colored smaller feathers of the inner wing.

***Tertials*** - Larger feathers of the inner wing.

***Vermiculation*** - Winding and wavy lines like the tracks of worms.

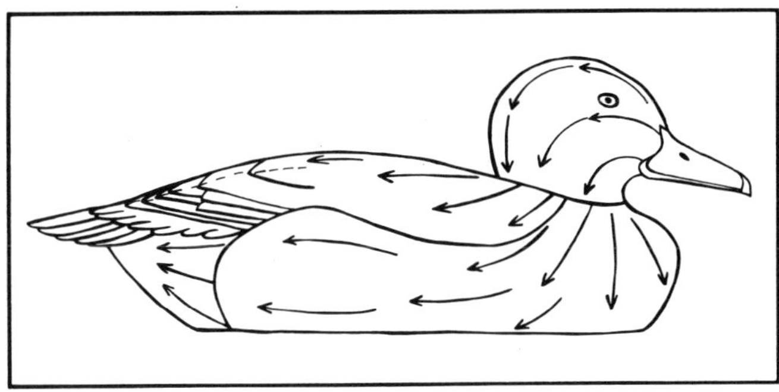

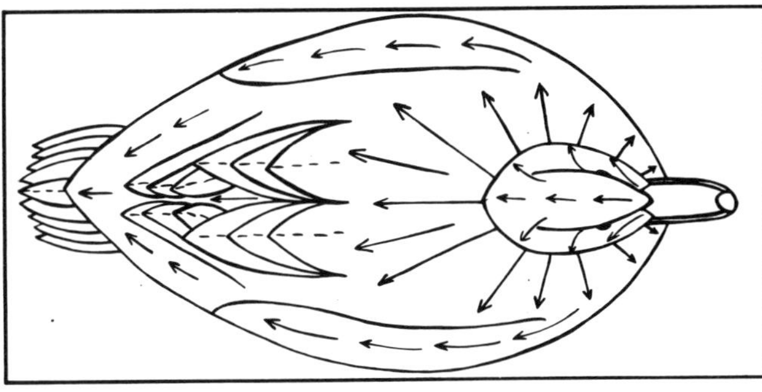

***Illustration #16***
*Feather contour directions (side and top view) are shown here for wildfowl species.*

## TIPS

**1)** Always keep your brushes clean! Wash them thoroughly with soap and water to remove *all* color, especially near the metal ferrule. Rinse the brush thoroughly and shape it with your fingers to form the natural shape.

**2)** Moths love good, natural hair, especially red sable. When you do not use your brushes often, please moth proof the storage area.

**3)** When using acrylics, a few drops of detergent added to the painting water helps to remove pigment when changing from one color to another.

**4)** Each coat of acrylic must be thoroughly dry before applying the next coat, whether it is a wash or regular coat of paint. If not, the wet coat underneath will come off and you will have an area to repair that takes both time and effort.

**5)** Permalba Acrylics will not hurt your red sable brushes, *if you keep your brushes clean!* Dried acrylic in brushes is almost impossible to remove. There is a product named *Goof-Off* which softens hardened acrylics. With several applications, working it into the brush, you can restore your old useless brushes.
Also, you can remove acrylic from fabric with a little effort using *Goof-Off.*

**6)** *REMEMBER!* The end of the feather always points toward the tail of the bird, otherwise, the feather will appear to be growing backward on the bird.

**7)** Painting strokes should follow the contour of the bird. The contour directions of the feathers of wildfowl are illustrated above. Illustration #16.

**8)** Feathers should connect, both front and back and side to side. No open "rows" of feathers should occur.

**9)** Collect reference material. Begin a library of bird books or any subject in which you are interested. Pictures from magazines, papers, and books are good sources to collect.

# RED HEAD DRAKE

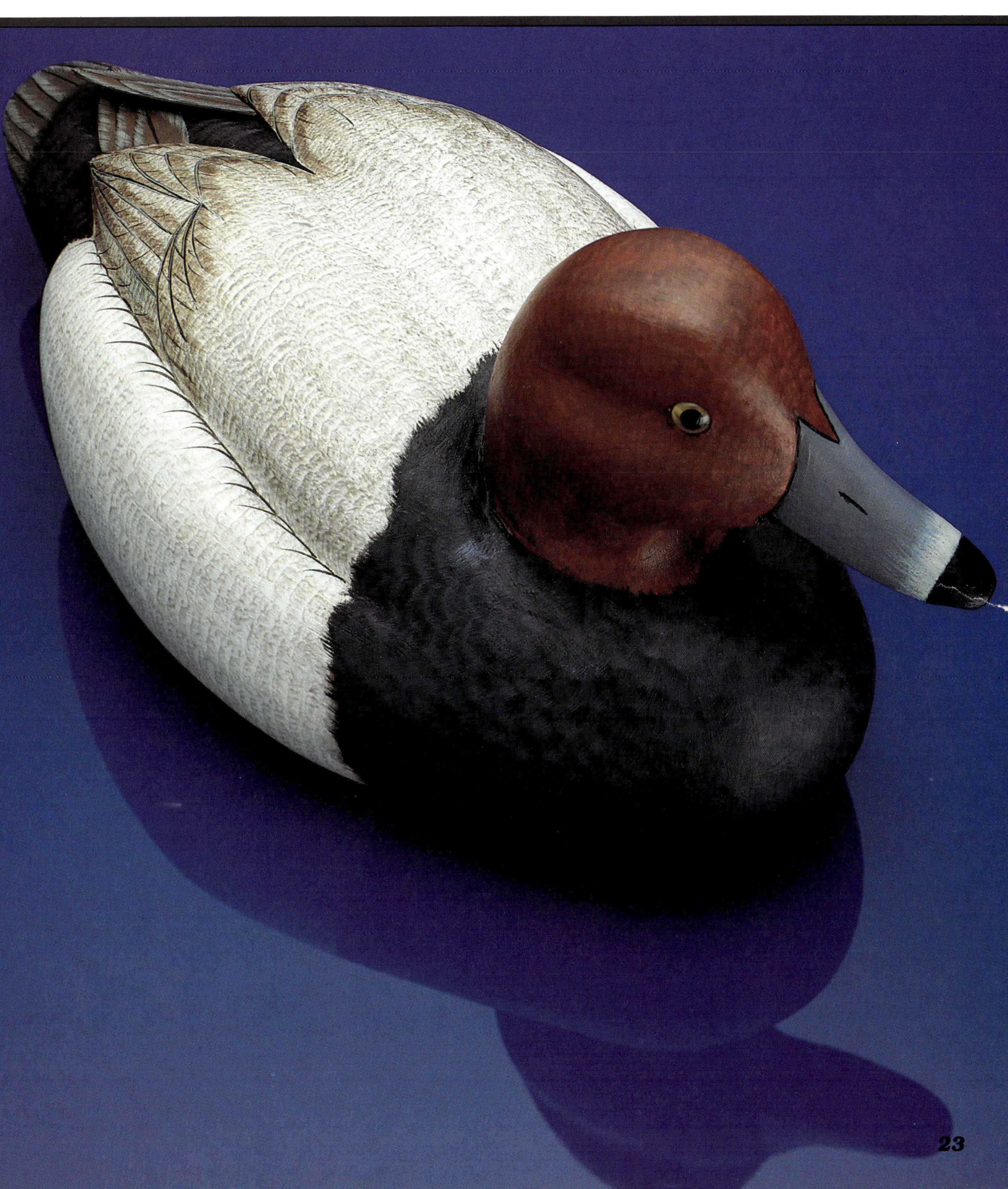

# RED HEAD DRAKE

**Permalba Colors**
Titanium White
Unbleached Titanium
Ivory Black
Raw Umber
Burnt Umber
Burnt Sienna
Paynes Gray

**Brushes**
Beebe Hopper Liner #0
Beebe Hopper Kats Tongue #12
Beebe Hopper Shader #10

*Burnt Sienna + Bright Red = Color mixture*

***Illustration #17***
*Shown above are color chips to create the mixture for the head area of the Red Head Drake. One part Burnt Sienna is added to one part Bright Red to achieve a rich, deep red tone.*

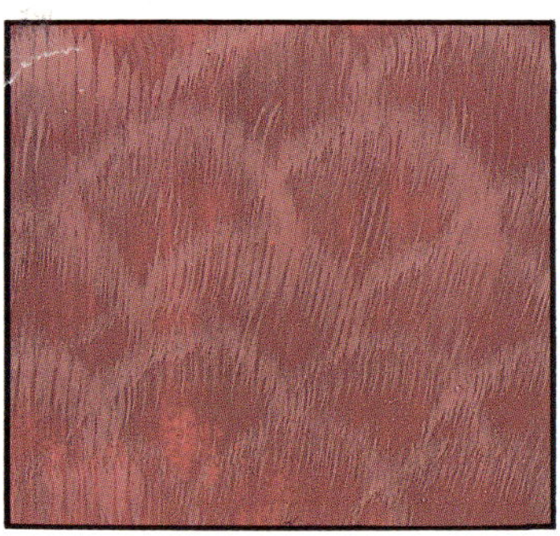

***Illustration #18***
*Feather pattern is placed over head area with a lighter mixture of the base tone red. Create this tone by adding a little Unbleached Titanium.*

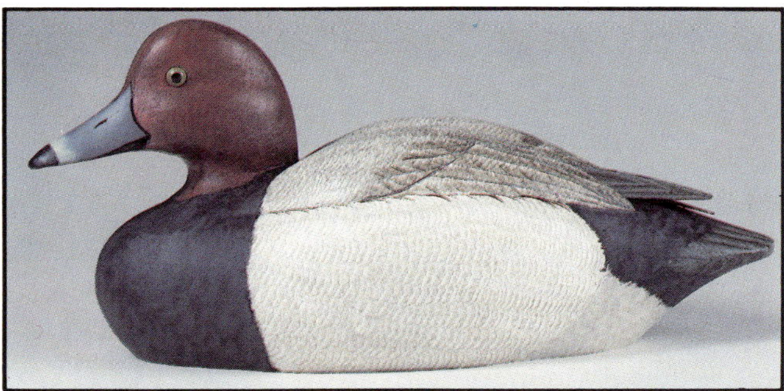

**Detail - *Side View***
*Note the feather placement and vermiculation technique on the side area of the Red Head Drake.*

Before beginning to paint the Red Head Drake, you should lightly sand the decoy to be sure it is smooth. Then apply a wood sealer to entire decoy and let dry. After the piece is sealed, apply a primer. Be sure primer is dry and lightly resand.

### Back and Sides

Vermiculate the duck's back and side areas, using method of your choice. For this carving, I used the matte medium method. See Section on vermiculation.

### Head

Mix one part Burnt Sienna to one part Bright Red to create the color mix for the drake's head. Refer to color chips - Illustration #17 and close-up photograph of the head. To create the feather pattern, mix a small amount of Unbleached Titanium into the red mixture so that color is just a little lighter. Using thin paint and a *light* touch, paint feather pattern over head and neck areas. Refer to Illustration #18. Apply a thin wash with a coat of Burnt Sienna-Red mix over the feather strokes. Using a Burnt Umber wash, slightly darken the crown of the head and the back of neck. Blend the Burnt Umber upward from neckline.

### Breast and Rump

Apply Ivory Black to the breast and rump areas. Several thin coats are recommended rather than one thick coat to achieve the dark color. Refer to color chips in Illustration #19. This gives more life to the color on the surface. For the feather pattern, mix a touch of

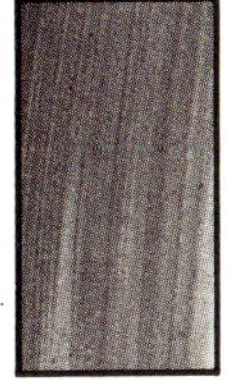
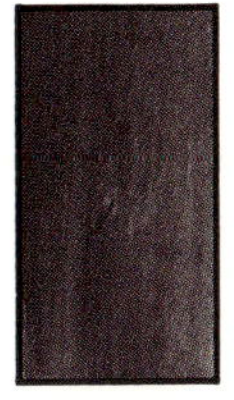

***Illustration #19***
*When applying Ivory Black to the breast and rump areas of the Red Head Drake, do so in a series of washes. Develop tone gradually shown in the wash stages above.*

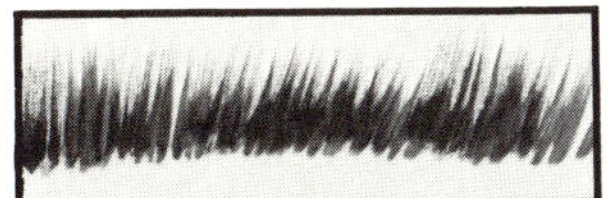

***Illustration #20***
*To avoid harsh lines at the neckline, feather out strokes creating a fuzzy edge to the Ivory Black color area.*

*Raw Umber + Unbleached Titanium = Color mixture*

***Illustration #21***
*Shown here are color chips to create the mixture for the primary and tail sections of the Red Head Drake. A touch of Unbleached Titanium is added to Raw Umber to make a dirty grey tone.*

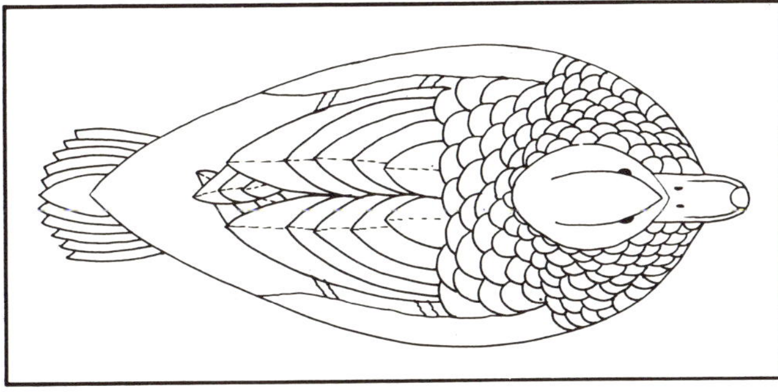

***Illustration #22***
*Feather placement diagram (Top view). Follow diagram for general placement of feather strokes on primary and tail sections.*

*Paynes Gray + Unbleached Titanium = Color mixture*

***Illustration #23***
*Shown here are color chips to create the mixture for the bill of the Red Head Drake. Paynes Gray and Unbleached Titanium are mixed to a medium value gray.*

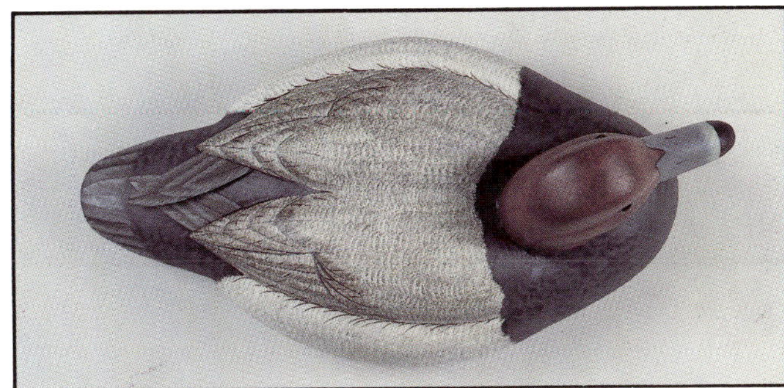

**Detail - *Top View***
*Refer to feather placement on the back area of the Red Head Drake, note how the vermiculation technique is achieved.*

Unbleached Titanium into Black to make a tone slightly lighter than breast and rump color. Brush on feather pattern using Beebe Hopper Kats Tongue brush #12 fanned to desired size. Follow the contour of body for the feather placement. Refer to general placement diagram, Illustration # 16 (Page 21). Blend in the edges to avoid a harsh division line at the neckline and at vermiculated areas. Refer to Illustration # 20.

## Primaries and Tail

Coat the primaries and tail areas with a mixture of Raw Umber and a touch of Unbleached Titanium. Refer to color chips - Illustration #21. Next, draw in the feather pattern with Black paint using Beebe Hopper Liner brush #0 for the fine lines. Apply feather strokes on the edges by stroking inward from outer edge with thin, soft strokes using Unbleached Titanium. Refer to close-up photograph of tail area and Illustration #22 for feather placement.

## Bill

Mix Paynes Gray and Unbleached Titanium to medium gray for base color of the bill. Refer to color chips - Illustration #23. Now paint nail area Black. Slightly blend Unbleached Titanium from the base of nail upward on bill. Refer to close-up photograph of the head for reference.

## Eye

Most carvings use glass eyes, but should you paint the eye, it is Cadmium Yellow with Black pupil.

# RED HEAD DRAKE

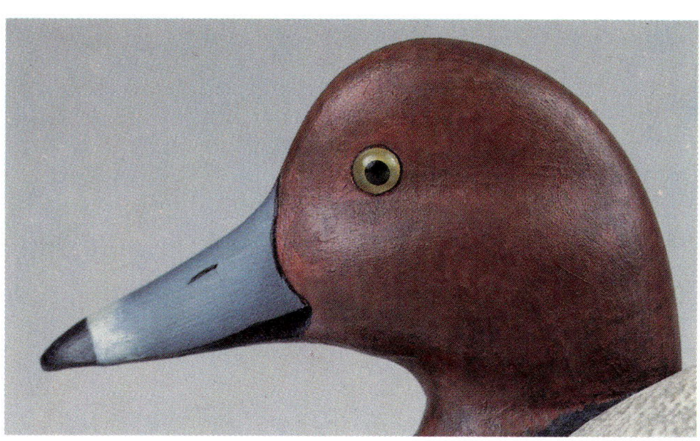

**Detail - *Head Area***
*The head area of the Red Head Drake is painted in an earth tone red with a subtle feather pattern stroked on.*

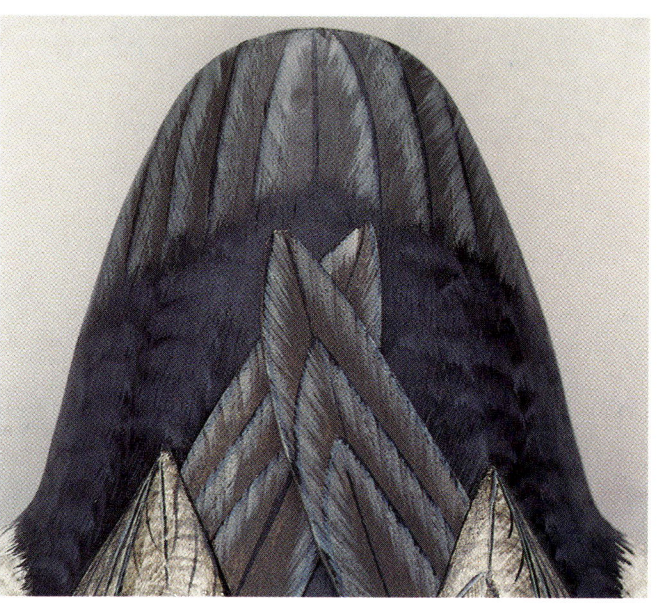

**Detail - *Tail Area***
*Pay close attention to the stroke direction of the feathers in the tail area. This section is painted in dark values.*

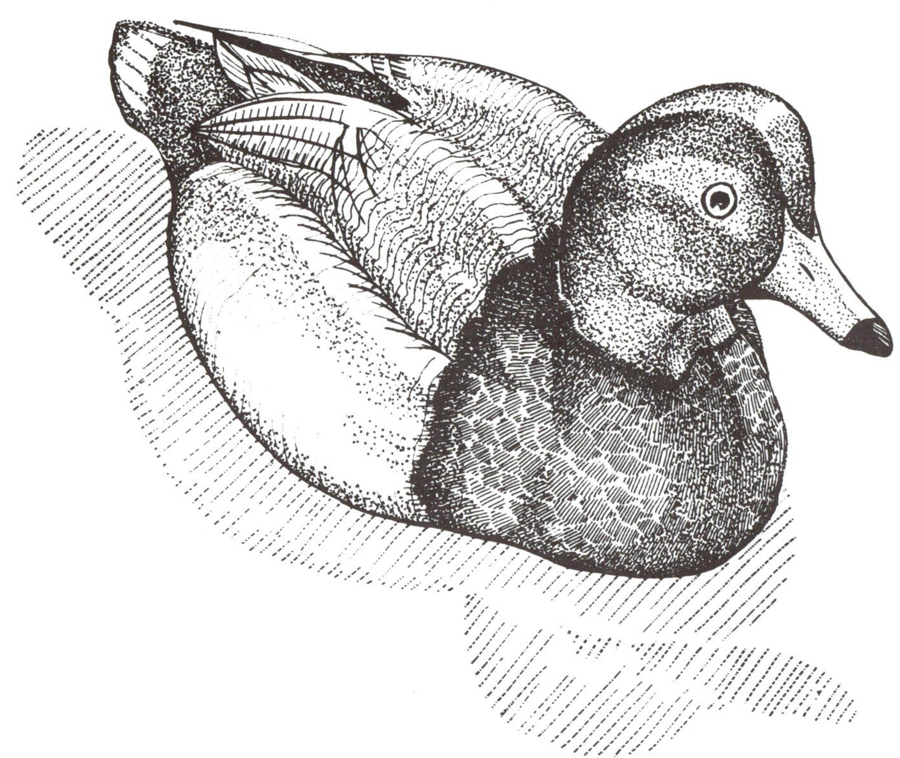

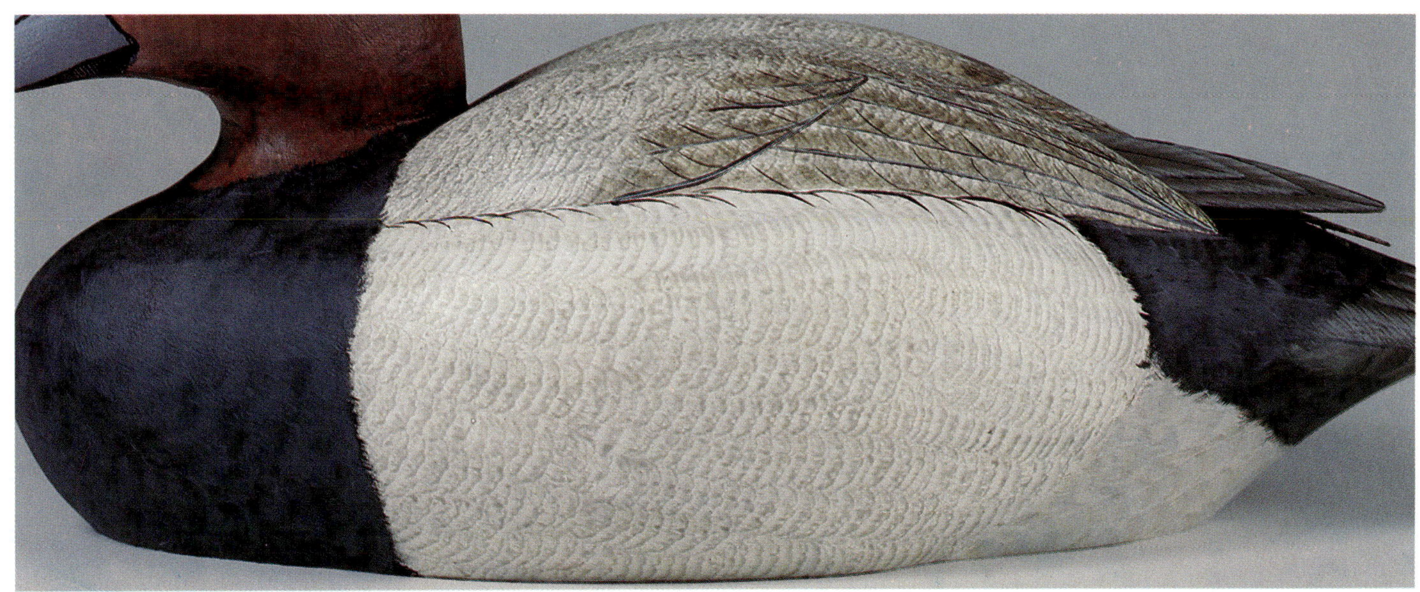

**Detail** - ***Side Area***
*Refer to this close-up photograph for stroking on feathers and applying the vermiculation technique on the side area of the Red Head Drake. Note the very dark chest area and subtle feather strokes.*

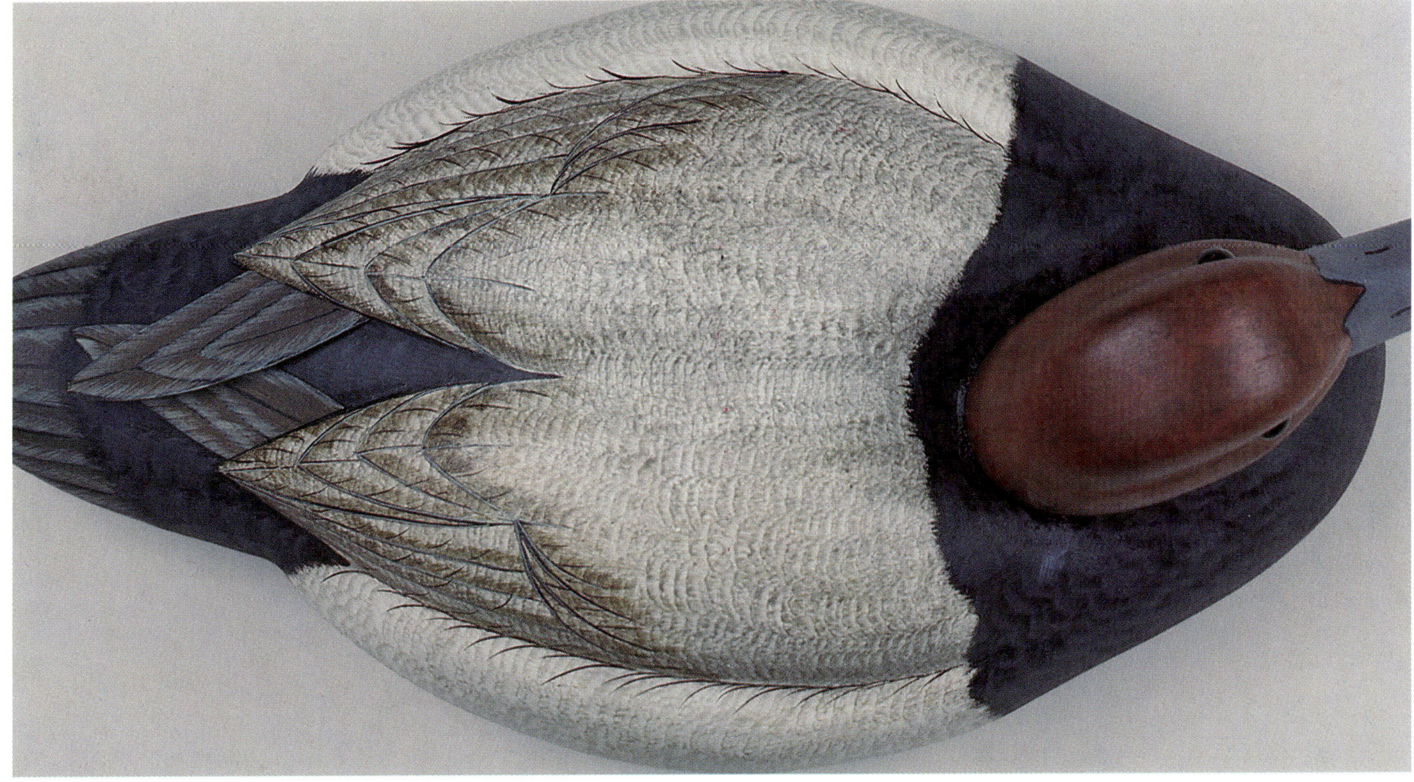

**Detail** - ***Back Area***
*The feather pattern on the back area of the Red Head Drake is achieved through the vermiculation technique. Note the darkening of the feather tips.*

# RED HEAD HEN

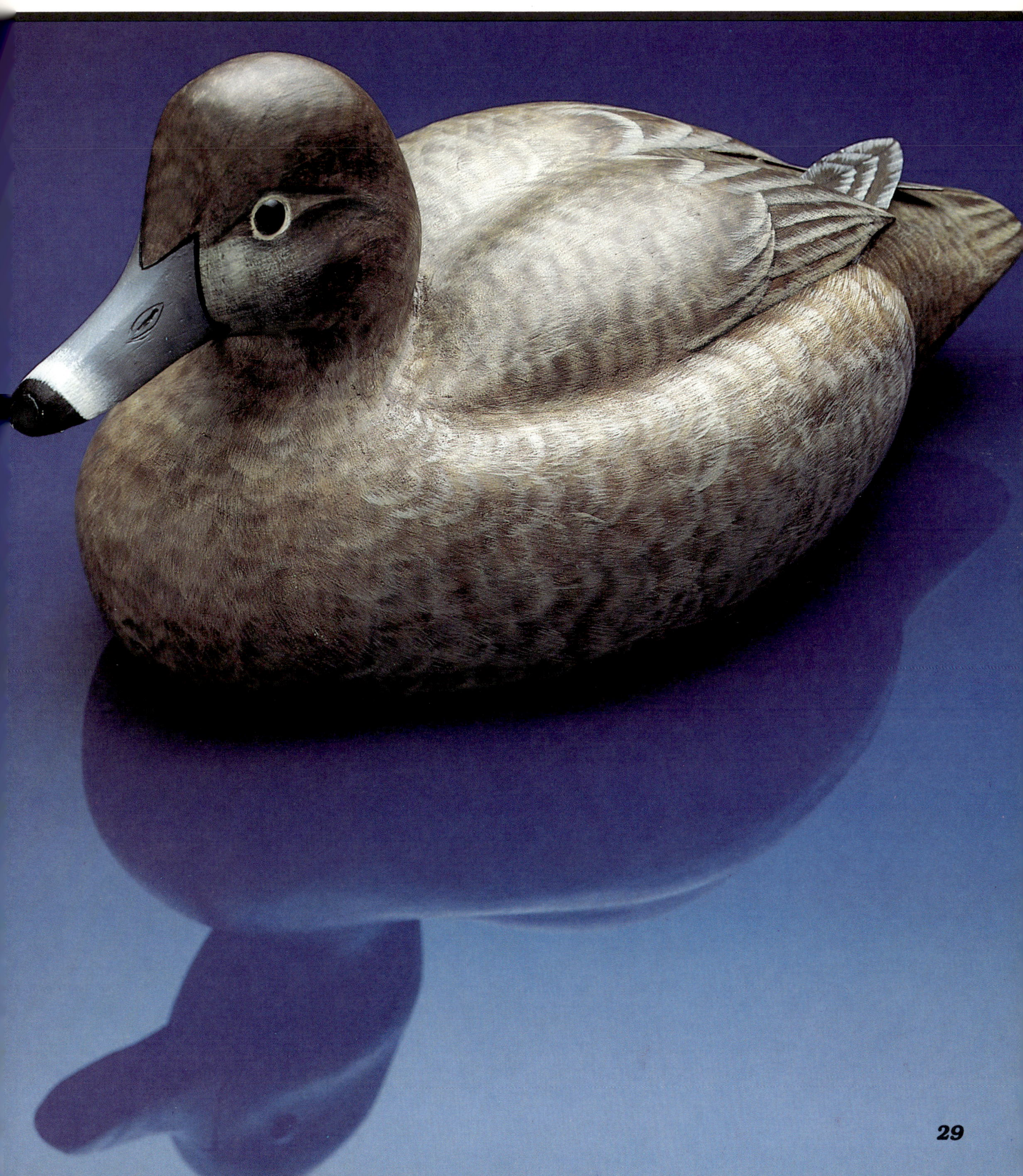

# RED HEAD HEN

**Permalba Colors**
Unbleached Titanium
Titanium White
Ivory Black
Raw Umber
Burnt Umber
Paynes Gray
Burnt Sienna

**Brushes**
Beebe Hopper Shader #10
Beebe Hopper Kats Tongue #12

*Raw Umber + Burnt Sienna + Unbleached Titanium = Color Mixture*

***Illustration #24***
*Color mixture for head, chest, sides and under rump. Created from two parts Raw Umber, one part Burnt Sienna and a touch of Unbleached Titanium.*

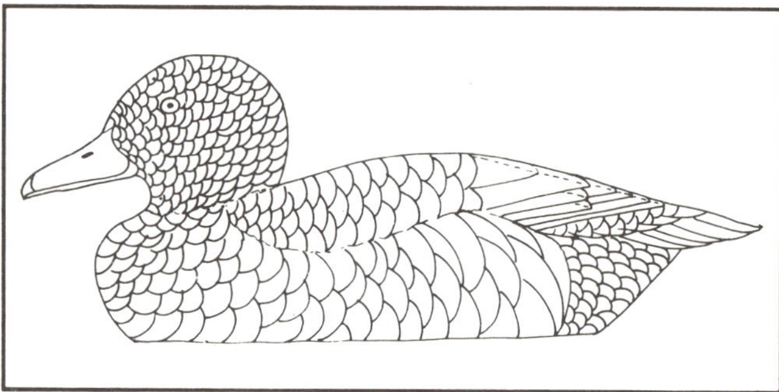

***Illustration #25***
*Feather placement diagram (Side view). To be used as a guideline for location of feather strokes on the Red Head Hen.*

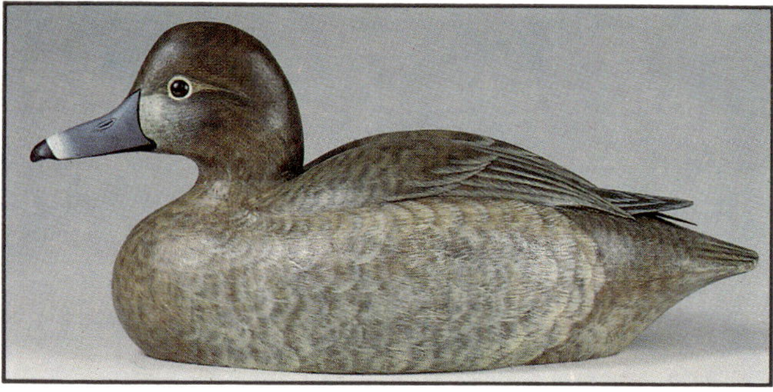

**Detail - *Side View***
*Note the feather placement and stroke direction on the side area of the Red Head Hen.*

Before beginning to paint the Red Head Hen, you should lightly sand the decoy to be sure it is smooth. Then apply a wood sealer to entire decoy and let dry. After the piece is sealed, apply a primer. Be sure primer is dry and lightly resand.

**Back and Top Rump**
Base coat with Raw Umber.

**Head, Chest, Sides and Under Rump**
To create a mix for the head and under rump areas, mix two parts Raw Umber to one part Burnt Sienna with a half part Unbleached Titanium to lighten the color. Refer to color chip - Illustration #24. Sides and chest are painted with a lighter color mixture of same, by adding more Unbleached Titanium.

Using the Beebe Hopper Kats Tongue brush #12 and Unbleached Titanium, paint the feather pattern over entire bird referring to Illustration #25 and #26 for feather layout. Reduce size of brush by pinching the brush with your fingers to paint the areas with smaller feathers. Apply a wash of Raw Umber on the back, head, and rump areas. Apply a wash of Burnt Umber on the sides and chest. Continue the layers of feather patterns and washes until desired softness is achieved. Refer to Illustration #27.

**Primaries, Secondaries and Tail**
Using feather layout, draw in feathers over the painted surface for the primaries, secondaries and tail. Paint these areas with a thin coat of Raw Umber. From the outer edge, stroke inward with Unbleached Titanium using the Beebe Hopper Shader brush #10. Apply these strokes on with a very light touch.

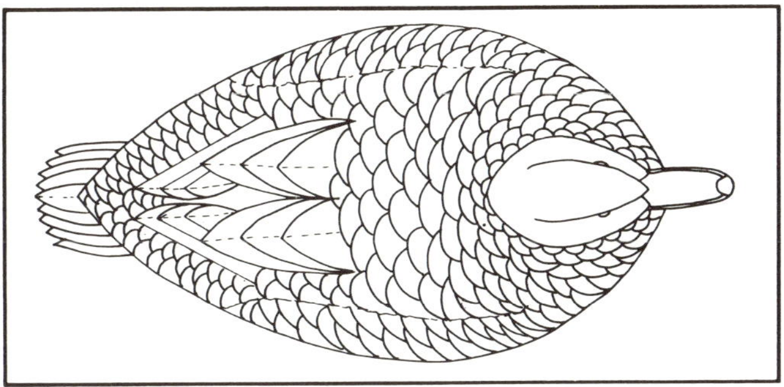

***Illustration #26***
*Feather placement diagram (Top view). Follow diagram for general placement of feather strokes on the back and tail sections of the Red Head Hen.*

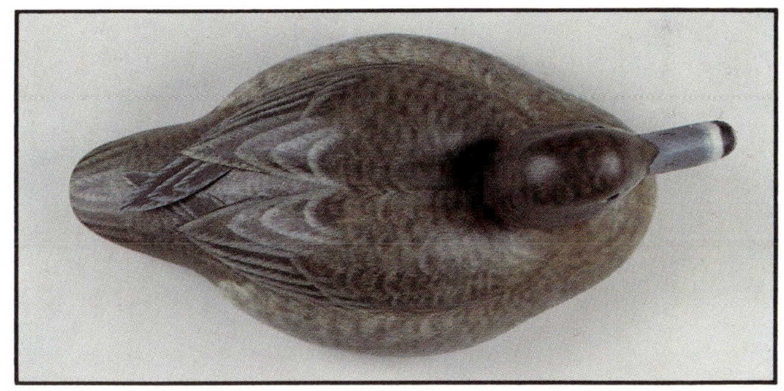

**Detail - *Top View***
*Refer to feather placement on the back area of the Red Head Hen, note the stronger areas of light on the feather edges.*

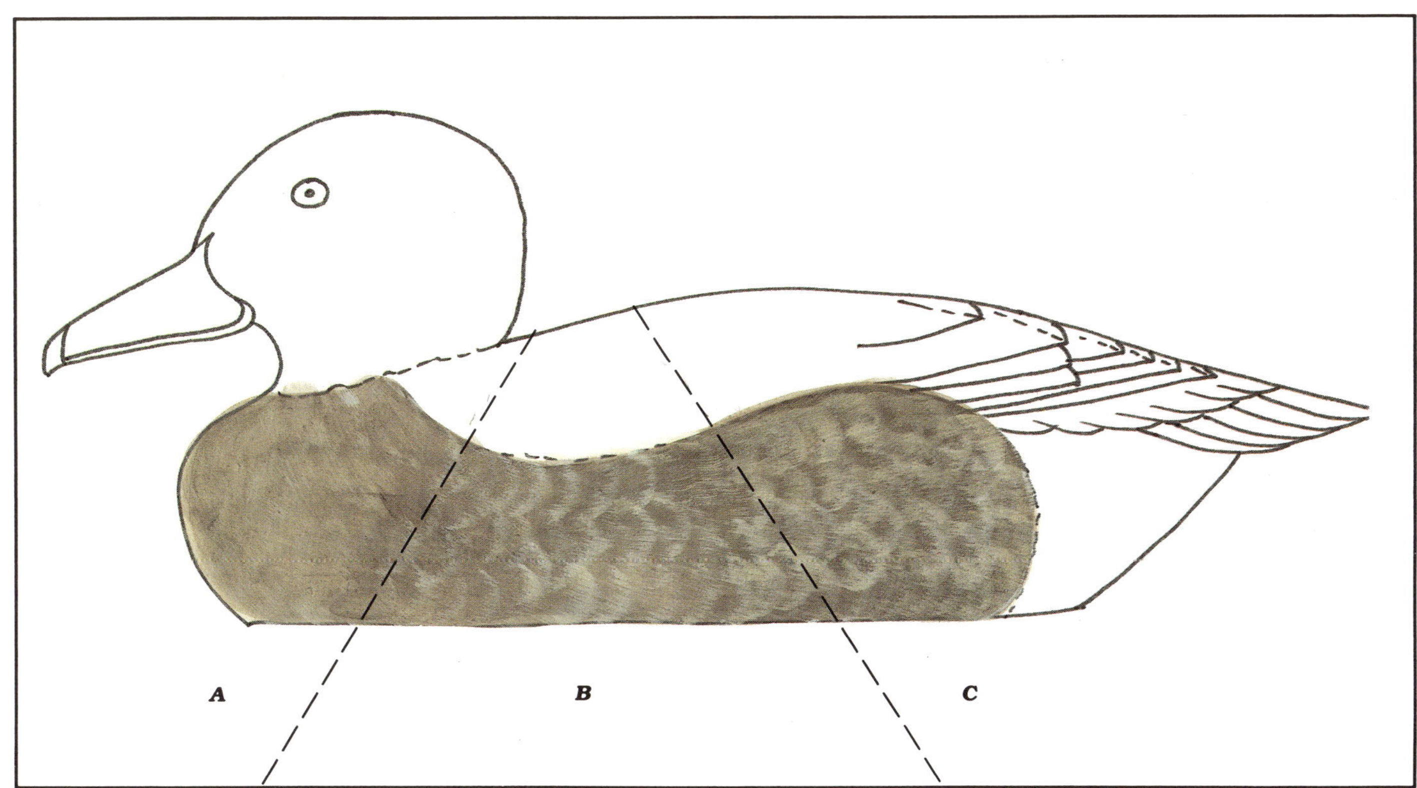


***Illustration #27***
*Shown above is feather development through stages on chest and side areas of the Red Head Hen. In Section A, one feather stroke pattern has been placed on with Unbleached Titanium and one wash of Burnt Umber. Section B has two layers of feather strokes in Unbleached Titanium and two washes of Burnt Umber applied. In Section C, three layers of feather strokes and three color washes have been applied to create the layered look of feather dimension.*

**Bill**

Basecoat the bill with a medium gray mixture of Unbleached Titanium and Paynes Gray. Paint the tip of bill in Black. Stroke inward from the Black area with Unbleached Titanium.

**Cheeks**

*Lightly* shade the cheeks inward from bill area with Unbleached Titanium. Stroke from the edge and towards the end of the stroke apply a light pressure and lift up.

**Eye**

Base the eye in Burnt Umber if not using a glass eye.

**Eye Ring**

Place a ring of Unbleached Titanium around the eye area.

# RED HEAD HEN

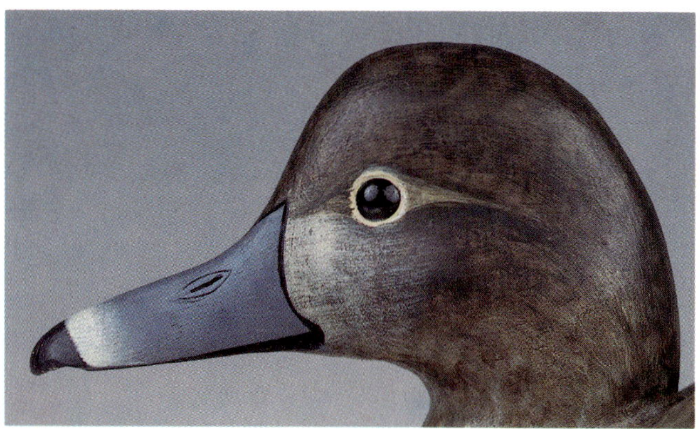

**Detail - *Head Area***
*The head area of the Red Head Hen is quite dark, the lightest area is below the eye, stroked from the beak area. Note the eye trough painted in a light value.*

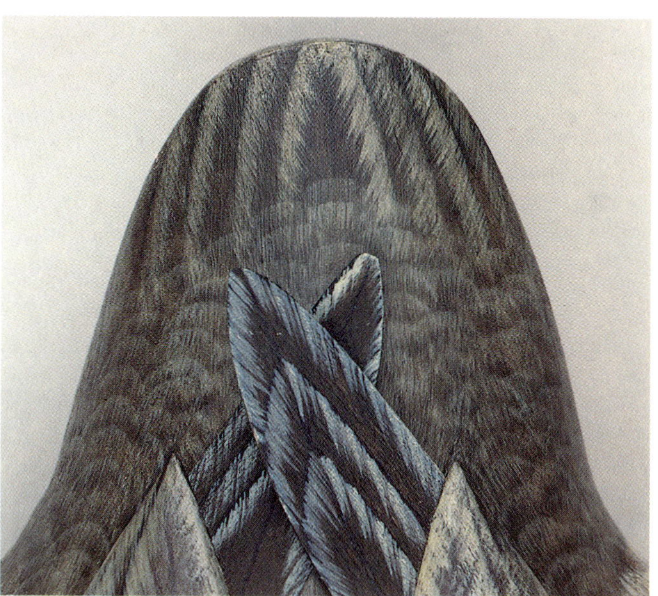

**Detail - *Tail Area***
*Take note of the stroke direction of the feathers in the tail area. The values from light to dark are fairly subdued.*

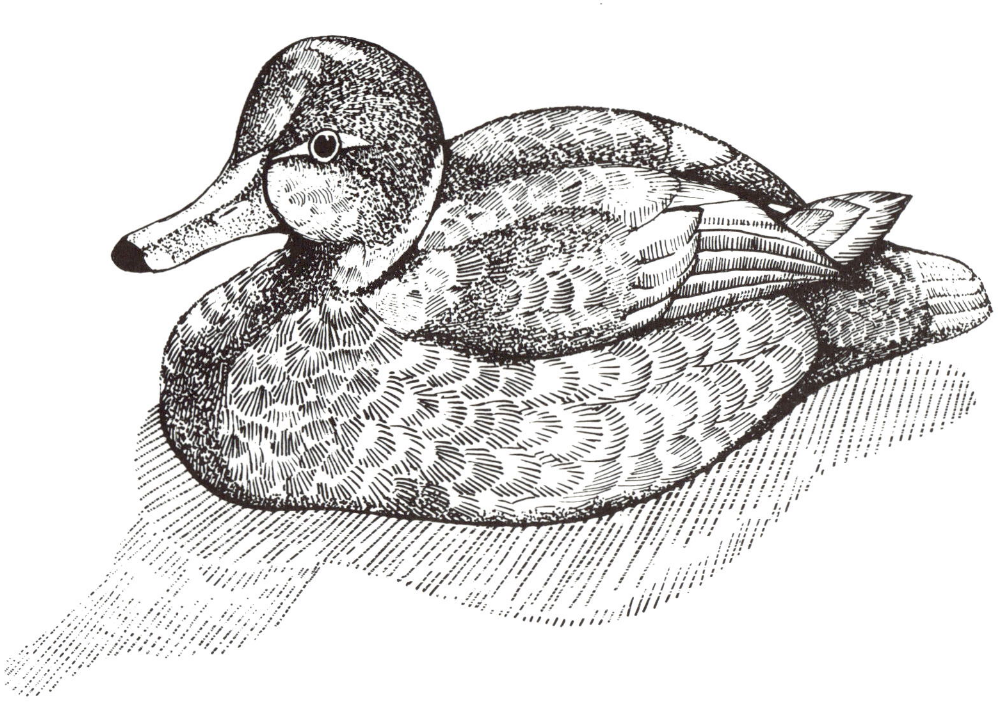

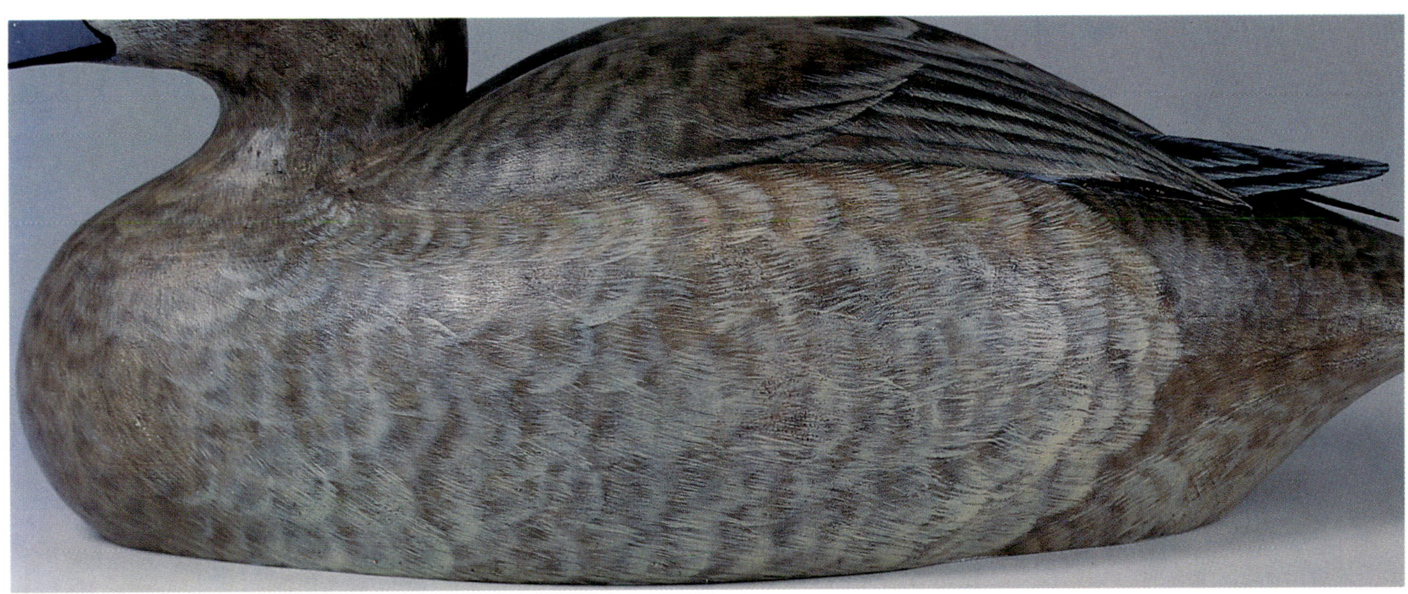

**Detail** - ***Side Area***

*Refer to this close-up photograph for stroking on feathers on the side area of the Red Head Hen. Note the feathers that are receding to the right are lighter in value.*

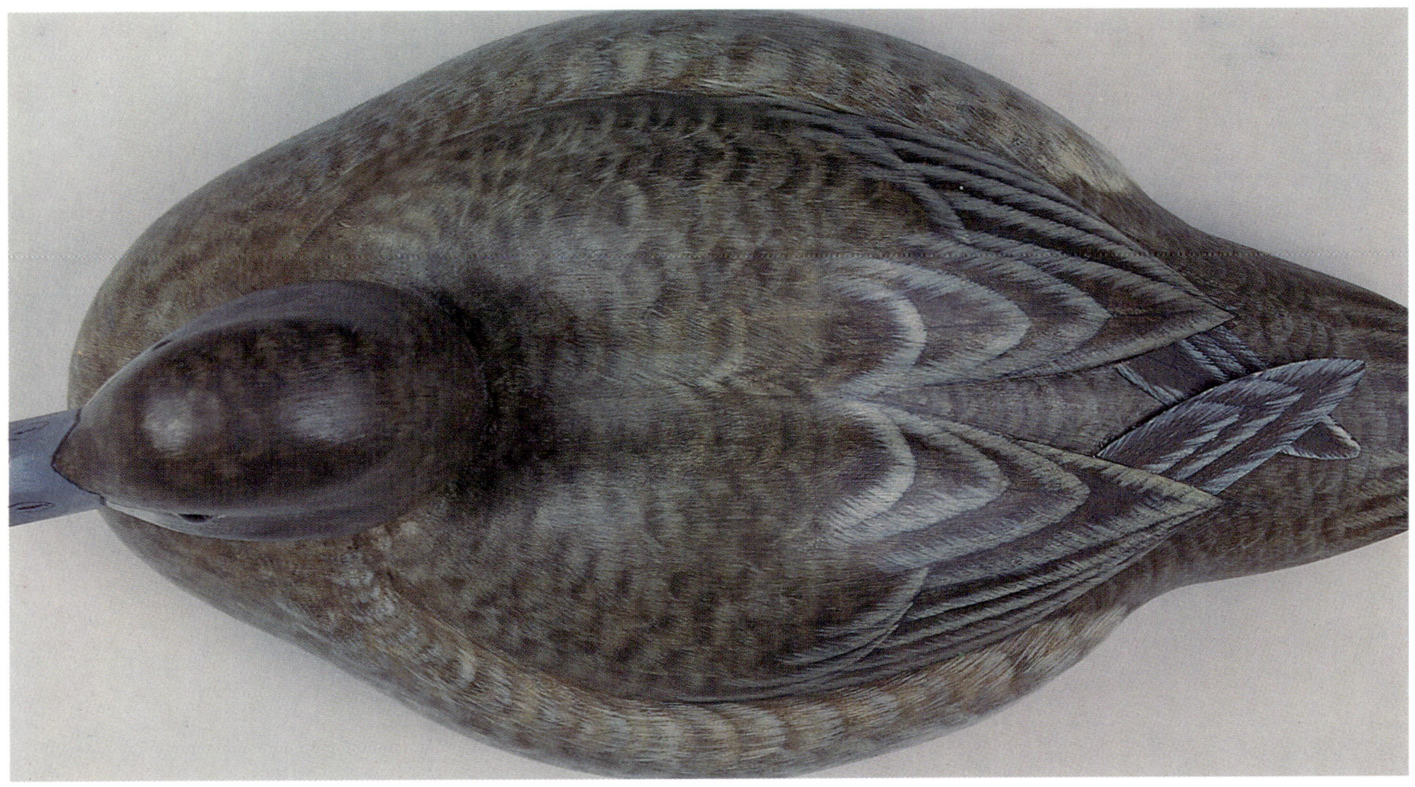

**Detail** - ***Back Area***

*The feather pattern on the back area of the Red Head Hen is very subtle. Tones of the feathers blend softly, achieved through a series of washes.*

# MALLARD DRAKE

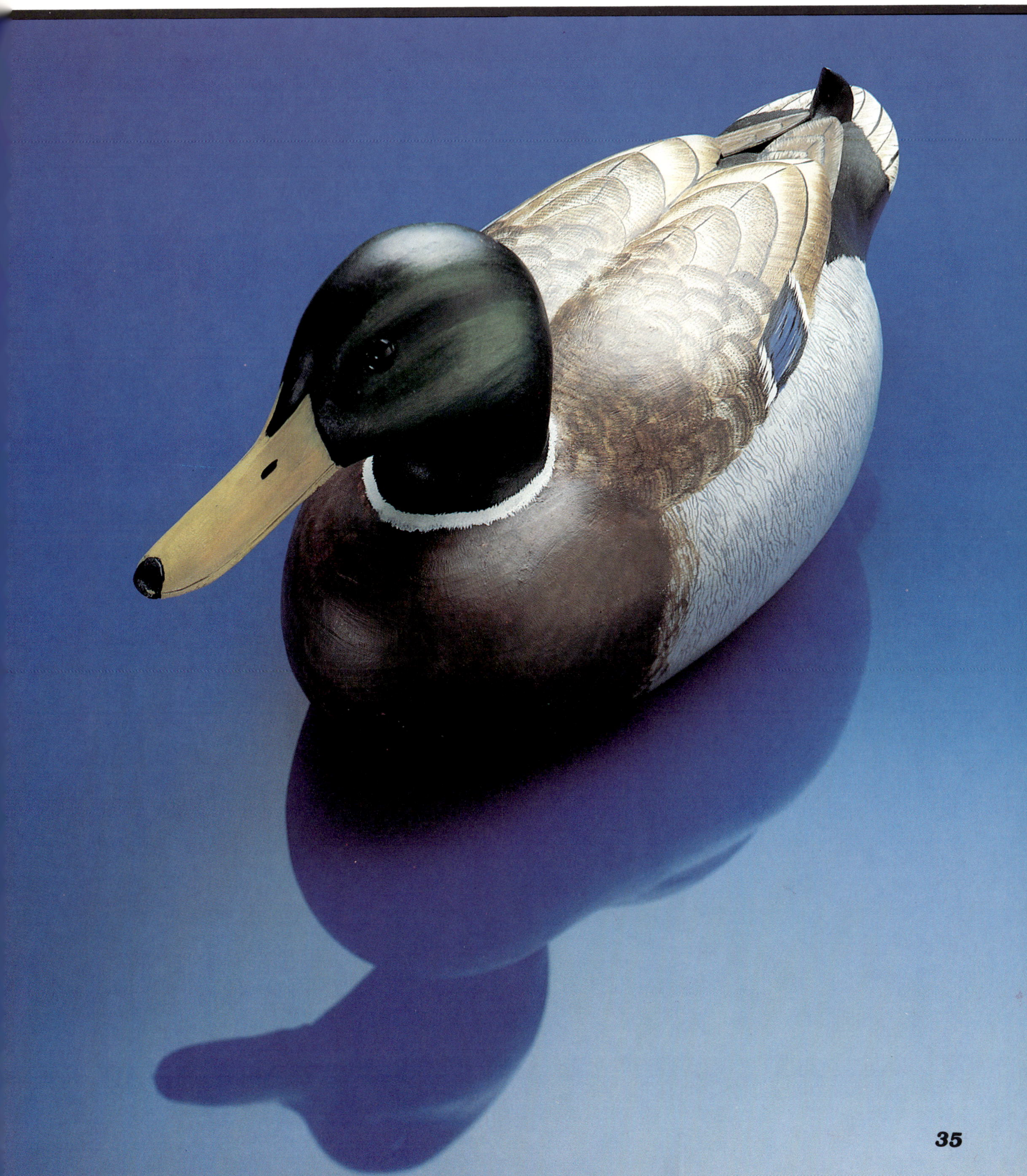

# MALLARD DRAKE

**Permalba Colors**
Titanium White
Unbleached Titanium
Black
Raw Umber
Burnt Umber
Burnt Sienna
Hookers Green
Cadmium Yellow Medium
Iridescent Green or Gold
Ultramarine Blue

**Brushes**
Beebe Hopper Liner #0
Beebe Hopper Shader #10
Beebe Hopper Kats Tongue #12

*Unbleached Titanium + Ivory Black = Color Mixture*

***Illustration #28***
*Shown is the color chip of the mixture used to base the sides of the Mallard Drake. To make this mixture, add Unbleached Titanium to Ivory Black to achieve a medium value gray.*

*Unbleached Titanium + Raw Umber = Color mixture*

***Illustration #29***
*Shown above are color chips for the mixture to be used to base the back area of the Mallard Drake. Raw Umber is added to Unbleached Titanium to achieve a light warm gray.*

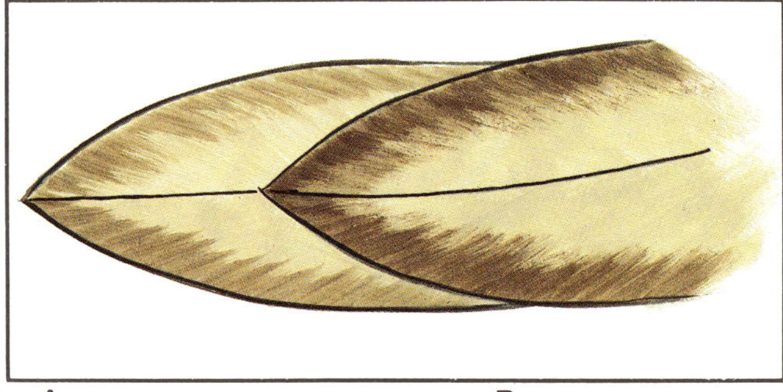


***Illustration #30***
*Feather pattern on back area of Mallard Drake is created in two stages. Section A shows feather shaded with a stroke of Raw Umber from the edge inward. Section B displays the feather overstroked in a Burnt Umber stroke from the edge.*

Before beginning to paint the Mallard Drake, you should lightly sand the decoy to be sure it is smooth. Then apply a wood sealer to entire decoy and let dry. After the piece is sealed, apply a primer. Be sure primer is dry and lightly resand.

**Sides**

Paint the sides of the drake with light gray made from a mixture of Unbleached Titanium and Black. Refer to color chip - Illustration #28. Apply vermiculation using method of your choice on the side areas of this duck. On the sides of the Mallard, I used the Beebe Hopper Liner brush #0 to create the vermiculation technique. See section on vermiculation for the details of application.

**Back**

Paint the back of the Mallard with a light warm gray mixture of Unbleached Titanium and Raw Umber. Refer to color chip - Illustration #29. Next, draw in the feather outlines, using the feather placement diagram as a guide. Apply lines with thin consistency Raw Umber and the Beebe Hopper Liner brush #0. When painting the tertials (long, elongated feathers), brush inward from the outside edge with Raw Umber. Lift up on the brush as you approach the next layer of feathers. Refer to Illustration #30 for color placement. Overstroke in same manner with Burnt Umber using the Beebe Hopper Shader brush #10. Use a light touch when feather stroking these colors.

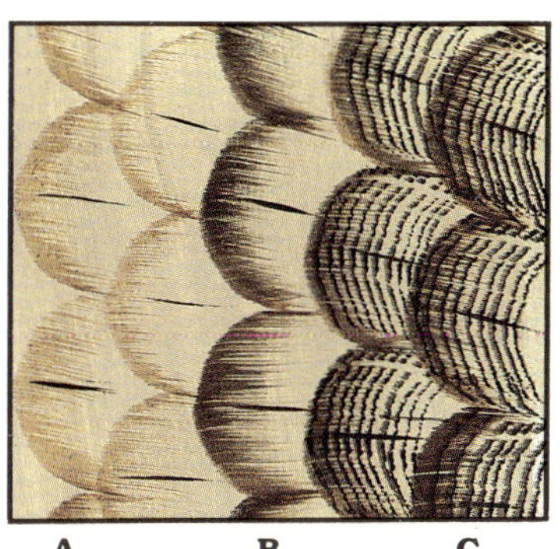


***Illustration #31***

*Vermiculation technique is shown here for the back areas of the Mallard Drake. Section A depicts the first step of the Burnt Umber stroke and the Ivory Black line down center of feather. Next, Section B shows a second stroke on the feather in Ivory Black. Section C shows vermiculation technique painted in Ivory Black.*

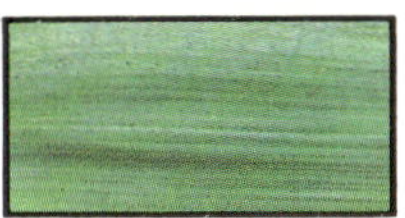

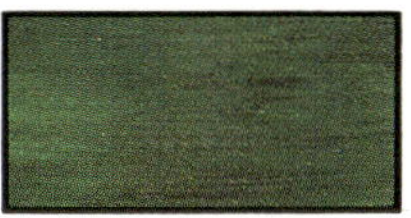

*Iridescent Green + Cadmium Yellow Medium + Hookers Green = Color mixture*

***Illustration #32***

*Shown above are color chips for the highlight mixture which is applied to the cheek area on the Mallard Drake's head. Iridescent Green is added to Cadmium Yellow Medium and Hookers Green.*

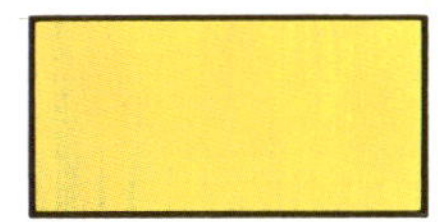

*Cadmium Yellow Medium + Raw Umber = Color mixture*

***Illustration #33***

*Color mixture for bill of Mallard Drake. Create a base tone of Cadmium Yellow Medium plus Raw Umber.*

***Illustration #34***

*Feather pattern is placed on the breast area of the Mallard Drake with a mixture of Burnt Umber plus Unbleached Titanium.*

## Shoulder

To paint the shoulder area, use the Beebe Hopper Kats Tongue brush #12. Create the feather pattern with Burnt Umber by stroking color on from the edge of the feather inward. Repeat feather strokes with thin consistency Black on top. Using the same brush and thin consistency Black, stroke arched shaped vermiculation marks on the three top tertials and shoulder feathers. Refer to close-up photo graph for details and Illustration #31.

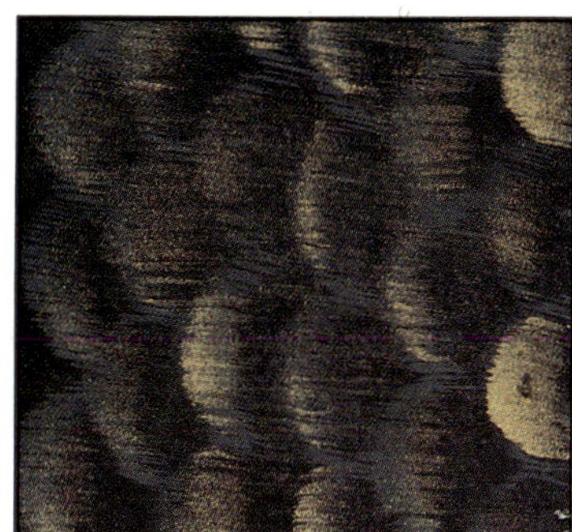

***Illustration #35***

*Top and under rump sections are based in Ivory Black and a feather pattern of Gold is placed on top.*

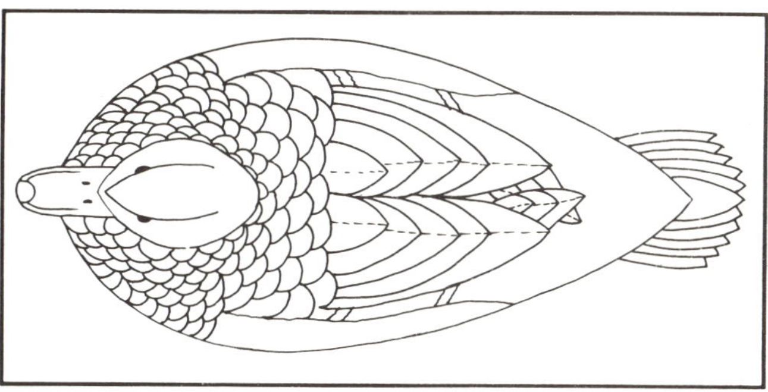

***Illustration #36***

*Feather placement diagram (Top view). Follow diagram for general placement of feather strokes on the primaries and other areas of the Mallard Drake.*

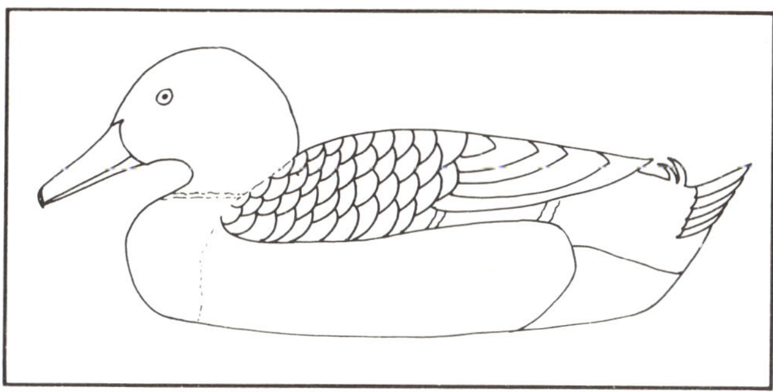

***Illustration #37***

*Feather placement diagram (Side view). To be used as a guideline for location of feather strokes on the Mallard Drake.*

## Head

Base the entire head shape with Hookers Green. To create the highlighted cheek areas, add a touch of Cadmium Yellow Medium to the Hookers Green base and blend into darker areas while the base tone is still wet. For an iridescence effect, apply Iridescent Green or Gold mixed with Cadmium Yellow Medium and Hookers Green. Refer to color chips - Illustration #32.

# MALLARD DRAKE

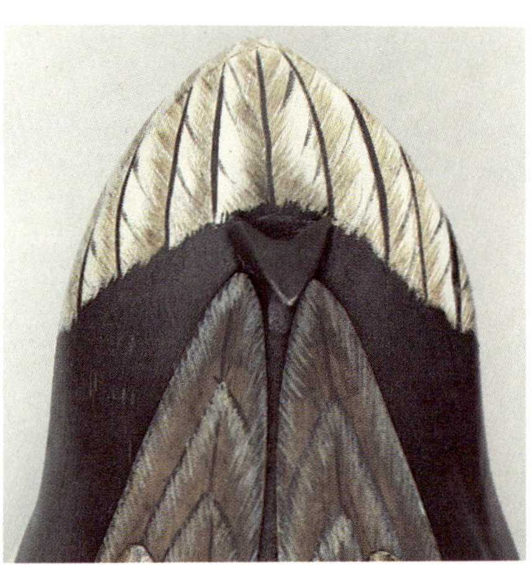

**Detail - *Tail Area***
*The tail of the Mallard Drake is an area of strong contrast between the dark black area and the off white tip.*

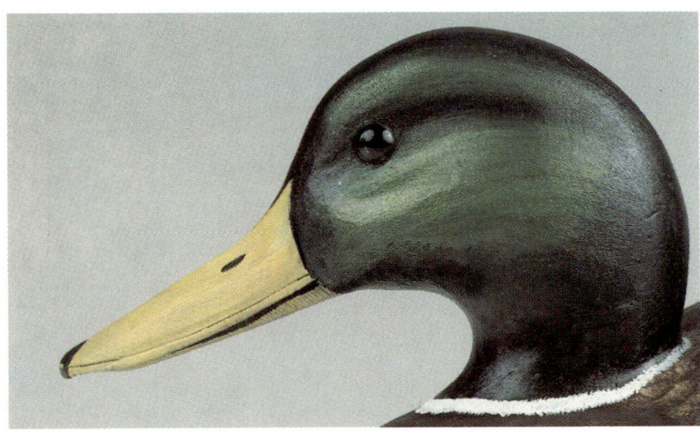

**Detail - *Head Area***
*The head area of the Mallard Drake is very dark in value with iridescent highlights on the cheek area and above the eye.*

### Bill

The bill of a Mallard Drake is the color of unripe bananas. To make this color mixture, add a touch of Raw Umber into Cadmium Yellow Medium. Refer to color chips - Illustration #33.

### Breast

Base coat the breast area in Burnt Umber. Next, apply thin Burnt Sienna washes until a rich chestnut color is achieved. To paint the feather pattern, mix a touch of Unbleached Titanium into Burnt Umber to make a tone slightly lighter than the breast base tone. Brush on the feather pattern using the Beebe Hopper Kats Tongue brush #12 fanned to desired size. Follow the contour of the body with feather placement. Blend in the edges to avoid harsh lines at vermiculated areas of the side sections. Refer to Illustration #34.

### Top & Under Rump Section

Apply several thin coats of Black to cover rump area. This will give more life to the color coverage than one thick coat. Stroke in a ragged edge to avoid harsh lines between sections. To create the feather pattern, mix a touch of Gold with Black to make a shade color lighter than rump area. Brush on the feather pattern using Beebe Hopper Kats Tongue brush #12 fanned to a desired size for feather strokes. Refer to Illustration #35 for stroke placement.

### Tail

To paint the tail area, you will need to mix one part Unbleached Titanium with two parts Titanium White. Let dry. Draw in the feather outline sections using a Beebe Hopper Shader brush #10, carefully shade with Raw Umber from inside area of the feather outward. Place all strokes on at the same angle. Refer to close-up photograph.

### Primaries

Base the primary feathers in with Raw Umber. Let dry. Draw in the feather outline sections. Highlight the primaries using the Beebe Hopper Shader brush #10 and Unbleached Titanium. Brush from outer edge of the feather inward with a soft touch and thin consistency paint. Feather strokes should always be directed at the same angle. Refer to Illustration #36 for feather placement.

### Speculum

Paint the speculum area in a mixture of Ultramarine Blue and a touch of Unbleached Titanium. Using the Beebe Hopper Liner brush, stroke in from each end with Black. Stroke in Titanium White edging inward toward Black strokes on each end. Refer to Illustration #37 for feather placement.

### Neck Ring

Stroke in the neck ring with a small flat brush using Titanium White. Blend and stroke outward on each side to avoid a straight white line.

### Eye

Base the eye in Burnt Umber if not using a plastic or glass eye.

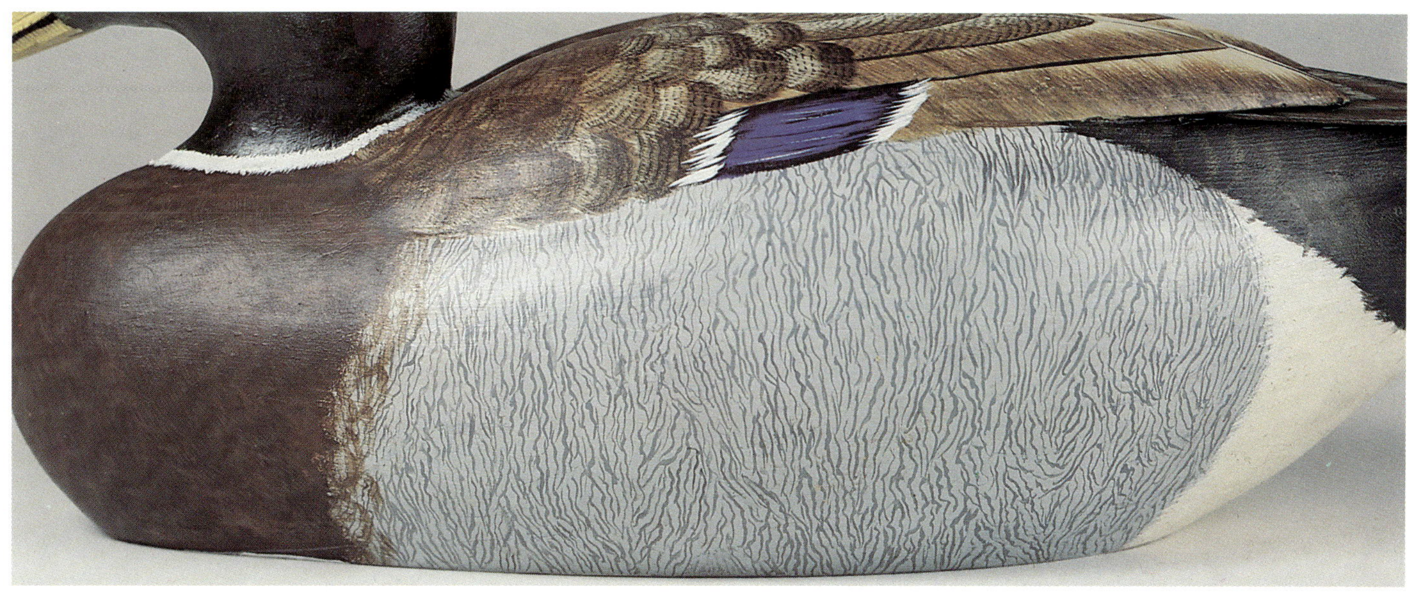

**Detail - *Side Area***

*Refer to this close-up photograph for stroking on feathers on the side area of the Mallard Drake. Note the linework vermiculation on the side.*

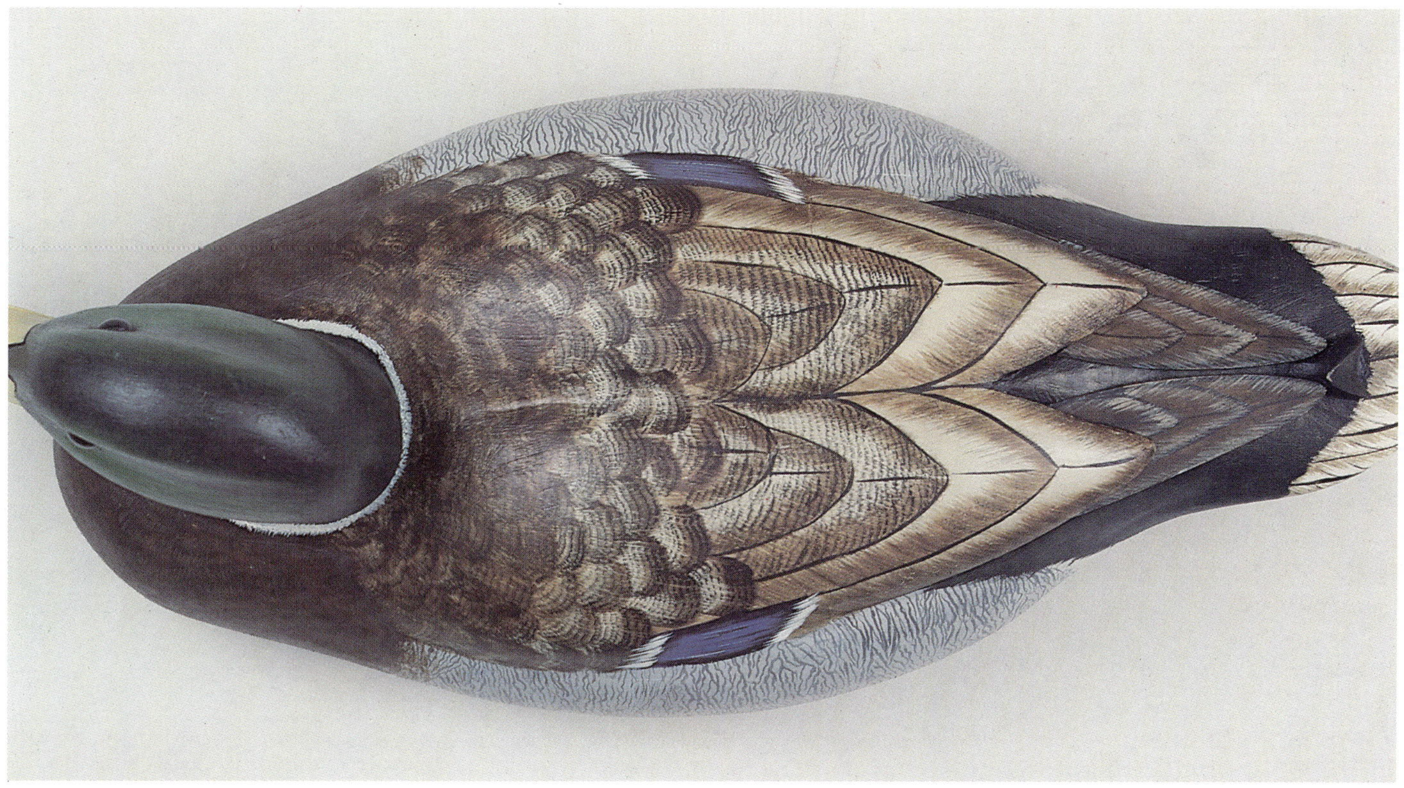

**Detail - *Back Area***

*The feather pattern on the back area of the Mallard Drake is varied in its distinct sections. Note the diverse feather shapes, created with feather strokes and vermiculation.*

# MALLARD HEN

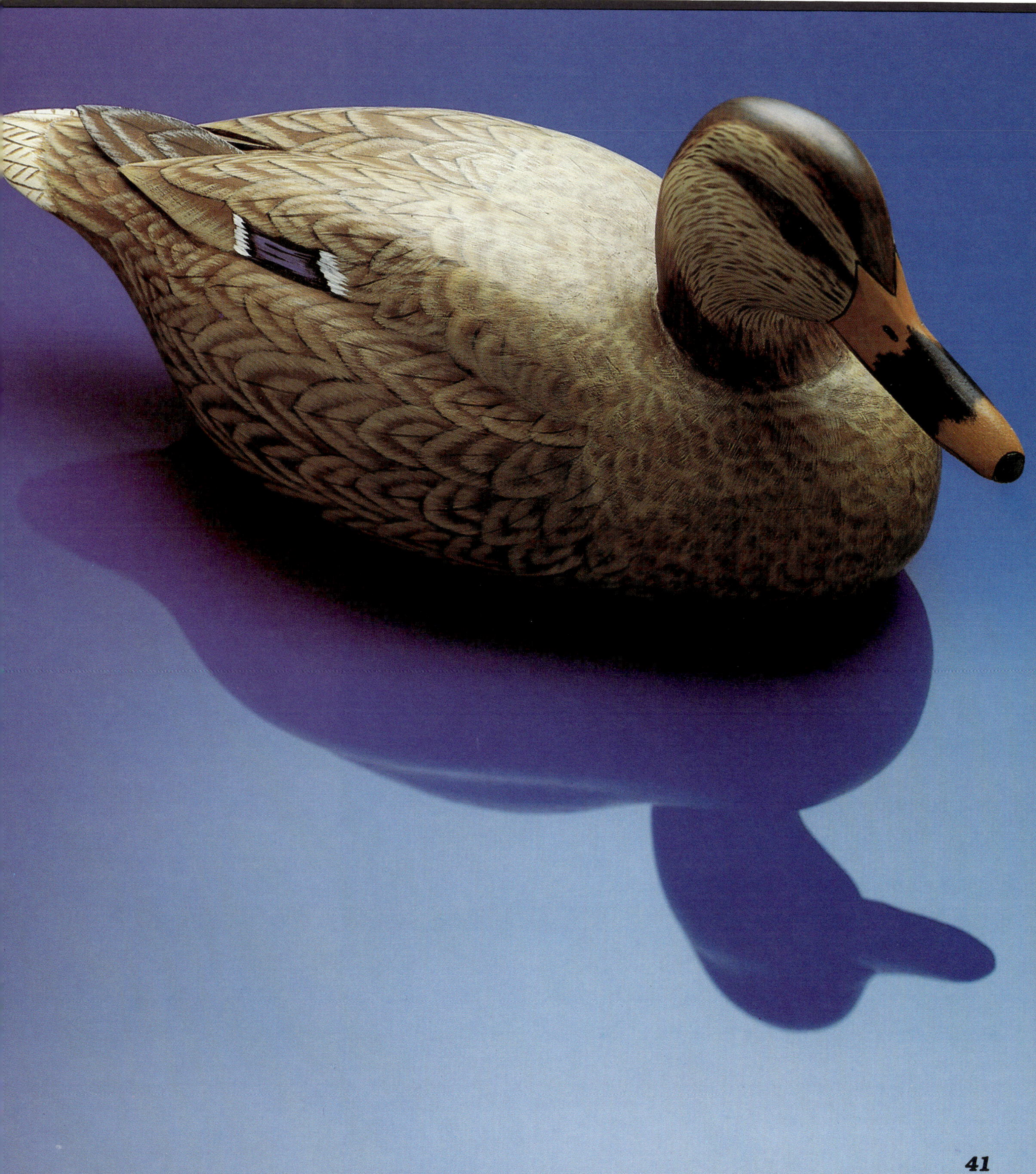

# MALLARD HEN

**Permalba Colors**
Unbleached Titanium
Yellow Ochre
Raw Umber
Burnt Umber
Ultramarine Blue
Cadmium Orange

**Brushes**
Beebe Hopper Liner #0
Beebe Hopper Shader #10
Beebe Hopper Kats Tongue #12
Beebe Hopper Shader #1

*Raw Umber + Burnt Umber + Unbleached Titanium = Color mixture*

***Illustration #38***
*Shown above are color chips for the mixture to be used to base the sides, back, rump, and chest areas. Raw Umber, Burnt Umber and Unbleached Titanium are mixed to create a dirty brown mixture.*

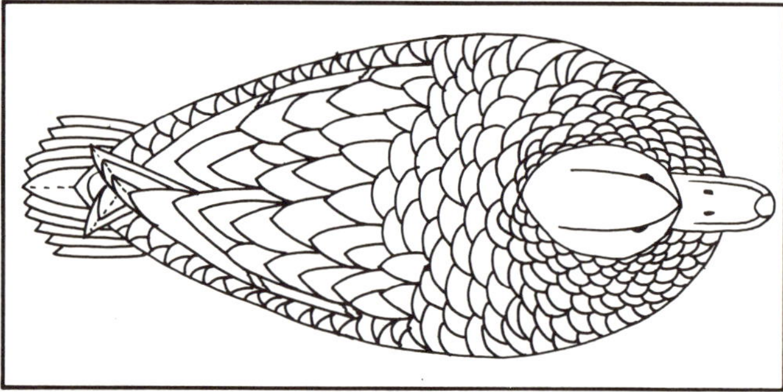

***Illustration #39***
*Feather placement diagram (Top view). To be used as a guideline for location of feather strokes on back and wing areas.*

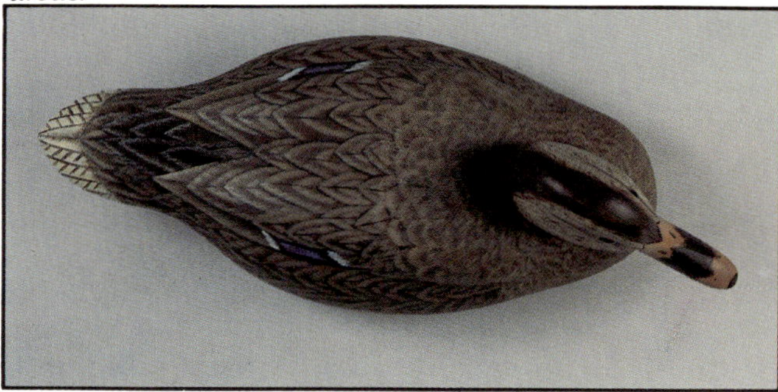

**Detail - *Top View***
*Refer to feather placement on the back area of the Mallard Hen, note the distinct sections of the feathers.*

Before beginning to paint the Mallard Hen, you should lightly sand the decoy to be sure it is smooth. Then apply a wood sealer to entire decoy and let dry. After the piece is sealed, apply a primer. Be sure primer is dry and lightly resand.

**Sides, Back Rump and Chest Areas**

To create a base tone for the sides, back, rump and chest areas, mix one part Raw Umber, one part Burnt Umber and one part Unbleached Titanium to achieve a dirty brown mixture. Refer to color chips - Illustration #38. Draw in feather outline using feather placement (Illustrations #39 & #40) as guide and using thin consistency Raw Umber with the Beebe Hopper Liner brush #0. Highlight the edges of elongated feathers using Beebe Hopper Shader #10 and a mixture of one part Yellow Ochre and one part Unbleached Titanium. The Mallard Hen feather has two highlighted areas, the second is half way down the feather section. Repeat the highlight color, placing it parallel to the light outer edge. Refer to Illustration #41.

**Breast, Shoulders and Rump**

Using the Beebe Hopper Kats Tongue brush #12 fanned to desired size, begin to paint the feathers. Stroke on the feathers using the highlight mix of Yellow Ochre plus Unbleached Titanium. After the feather pattern is painted over entire body area, apply a wash of thin consistency Burnt Umber. Repeat feather pattern application over entire bird and apply a second wash of Burnt Umber. Continue this

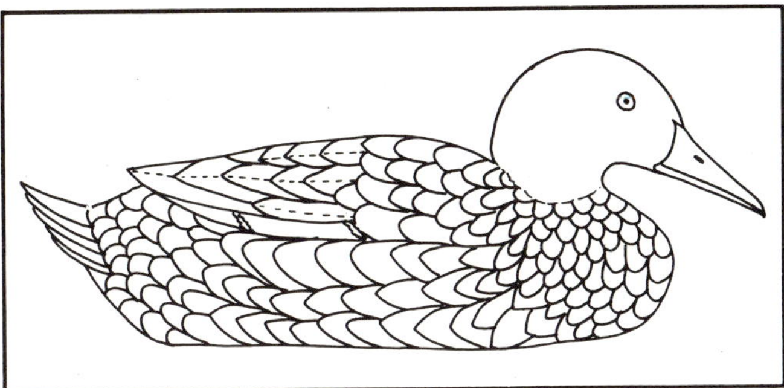

***Illustration #40***
*Feather placement diagram (Side view). Follow diagram for general placement of feather strokes on the sides, rump, and chest areas of the Mallard Hen.*

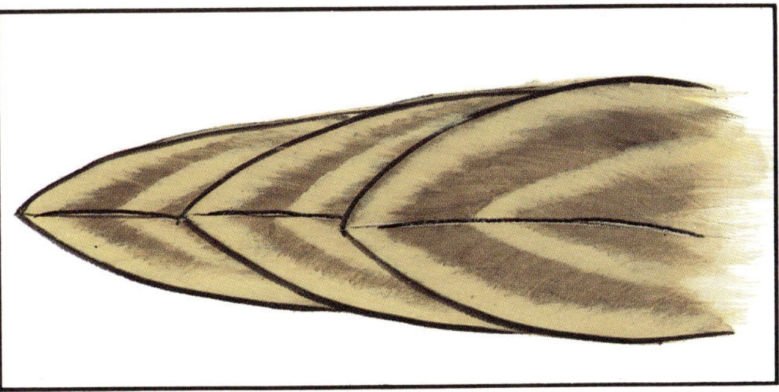

***Illustration #41***
*The elongated feathers of the Mallard Hen have two highlight areas. The second is applied at the half way point of the feather.*

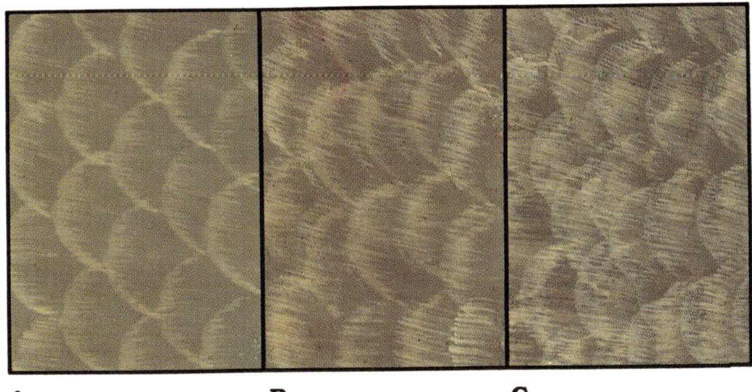


***Illustration #42***
*The feather pattern on the breast, shoulders, and rump is completed in a three stage development process. Shown in Section A is the initial feather stroke placement with one wash applied over the surface. Section B displays a second stroking of feathers and a second wash. Finally, in Section C, a third feather pattern and wash are applied to achieve depth in feather areas.*

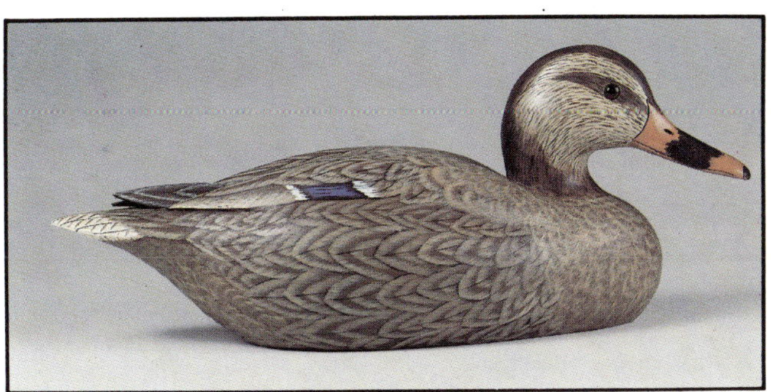

**Detail - *Side View***
*Note the feather placement and stroke direction on the side area of the Mallard Hen.*

process until desired softness of feathers is achieved. Refer to Illustration #42 for detail of color application.

### Head

Base the head in a light warm gray mixture of Unbleached Titanium mixed with a small amount of Raw Umber. Refer to color chip - Illustration #43. Darken the crown of the head and eye area with several washes of Burnt Umber. Soften the Burnt Umber division area by stroking up from the neck and down into the body area. Using the Beebe Hopper Shader brush #1 and Burnt Umber make a feather pattern on the head with short choppy strokes. Refer to close-up photograph.

### Bill

Base the bill in with a mixture of Cadmium Orange and a touch of Burnt Umber. Then Ivory Black is mottled into the center of bill.

### Primaries

Base the primary feathers in with Raw Umber. Draw in feather outline with thin consistency Burnt Umber using the Beebe Hopper Liner brush. Highlight the outer edge of the primary feathers with Beebe Hopper Shader brush #10 using a mixture of Yellow Ochre and Unbleached Titanium. Stroke from the outside edge inward.

Base the tail area in a mixture of one part Unbleached Titanium and one part White using a Beebe Hopper Shader brush #10. Let dry. Draw in feather outline with a thin wash of Ivory Black. Next, brush from the inside feather line outward with Burnt Umber for the feather markings using the flat edge of a Flat brush or the tip of the Liner brush.

# MALLARD HEN

***Illustration #43***
*Shown is the color chip of the mixture used to base the head of the Mallard Hen. To create this mixture, add Raw Umber and Unbleached Titanium for a light warm gray tone.*

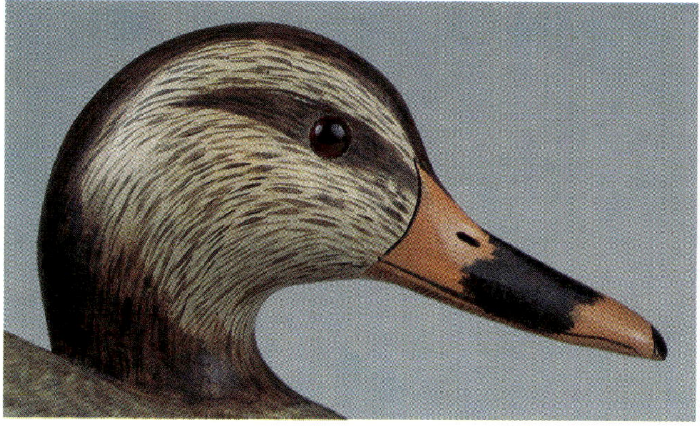

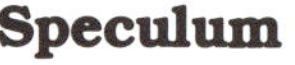

**Detail - *Head Area***
*The head area of the Mallard Hen has feather markings of strong contrast. Note the eye trough painted in a dark value.*

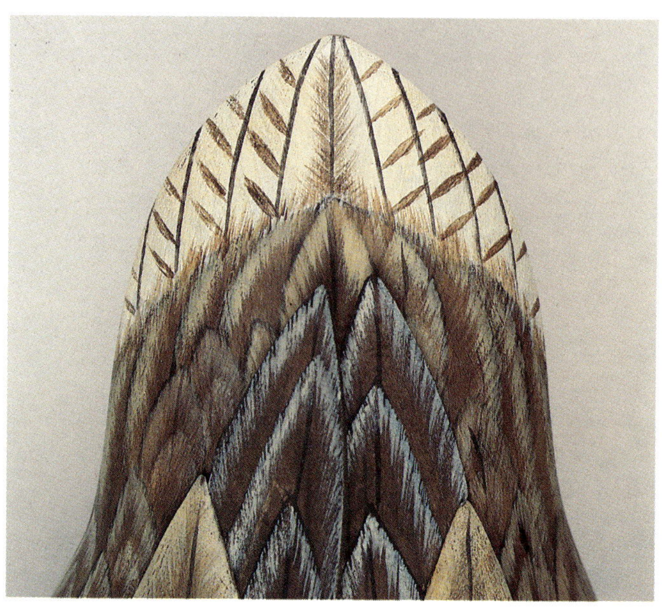

**Detail - *Tail Area***
*Take note of the stroke direction of the feathers in the tail area. The tip of the tail is kept light in color value.*

**Speculum**

Paint the speculum area in a mixture of Ultramarine Blue and a touch of Dioxazine Purple. Using the Beebe Hopper Liner brush, stroke in from each end with Black. Stroke in Titanium White edging inward toward Black strokes on each end. Refer to Illustration #40 for feather placement.

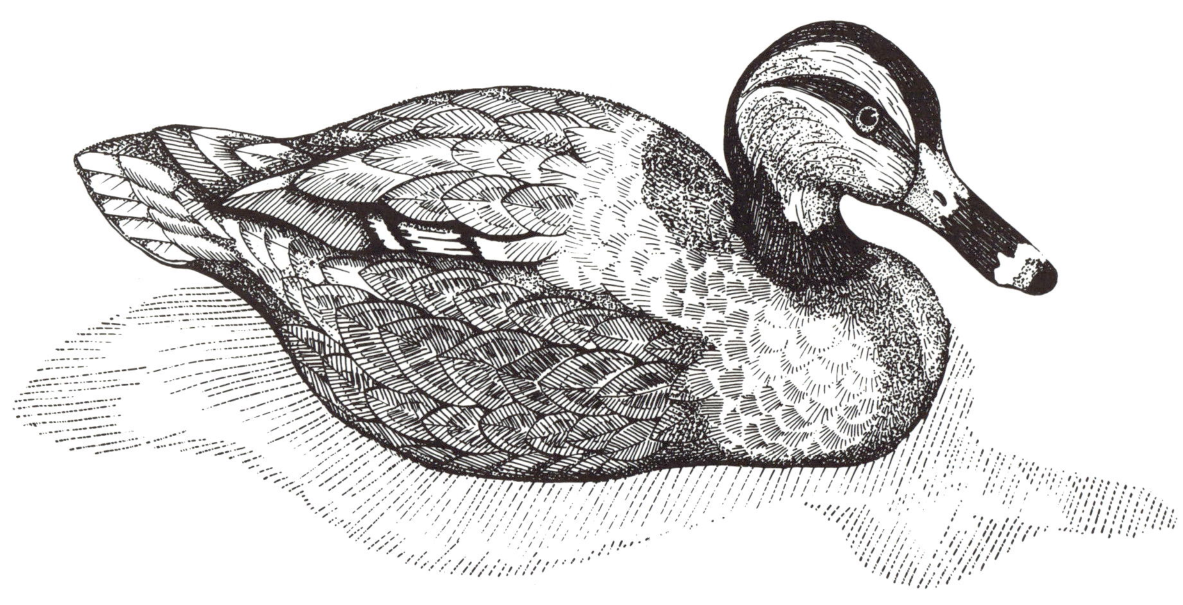

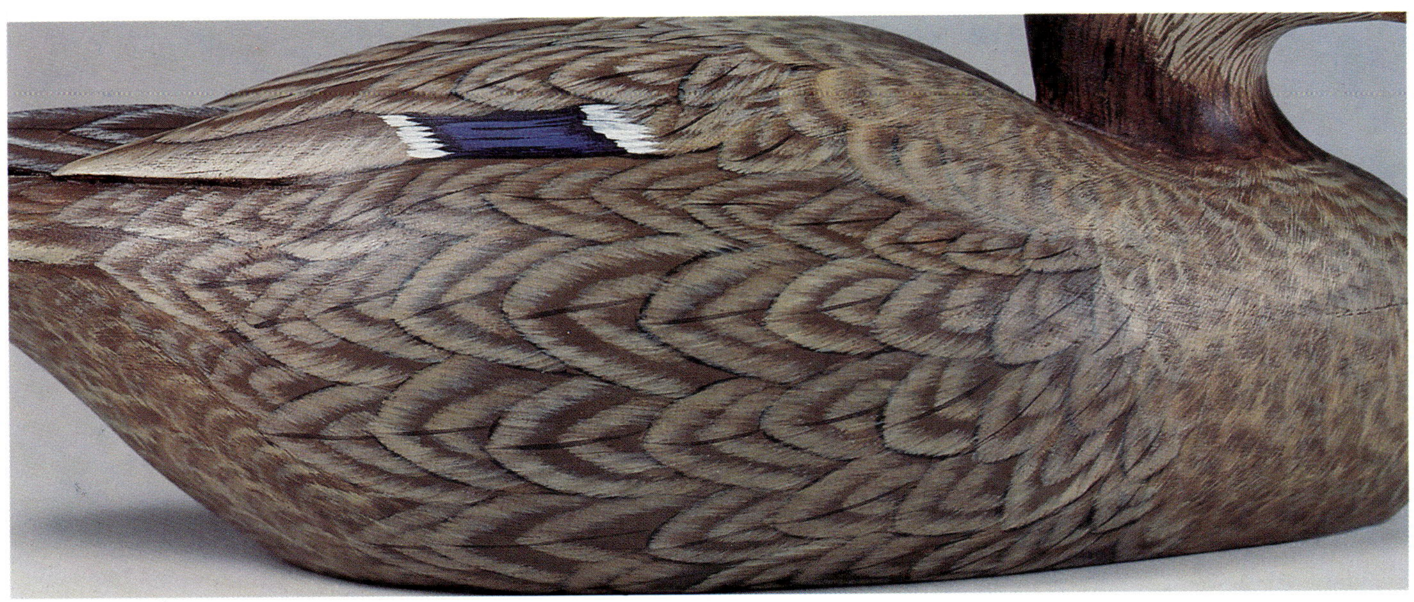

**Detail** - ***Side Area***
*Refer to this close-up photograph for stroking on feathers on the side area of the Mallard Hen. The feathers in this area are kept quite distinct and individual.*

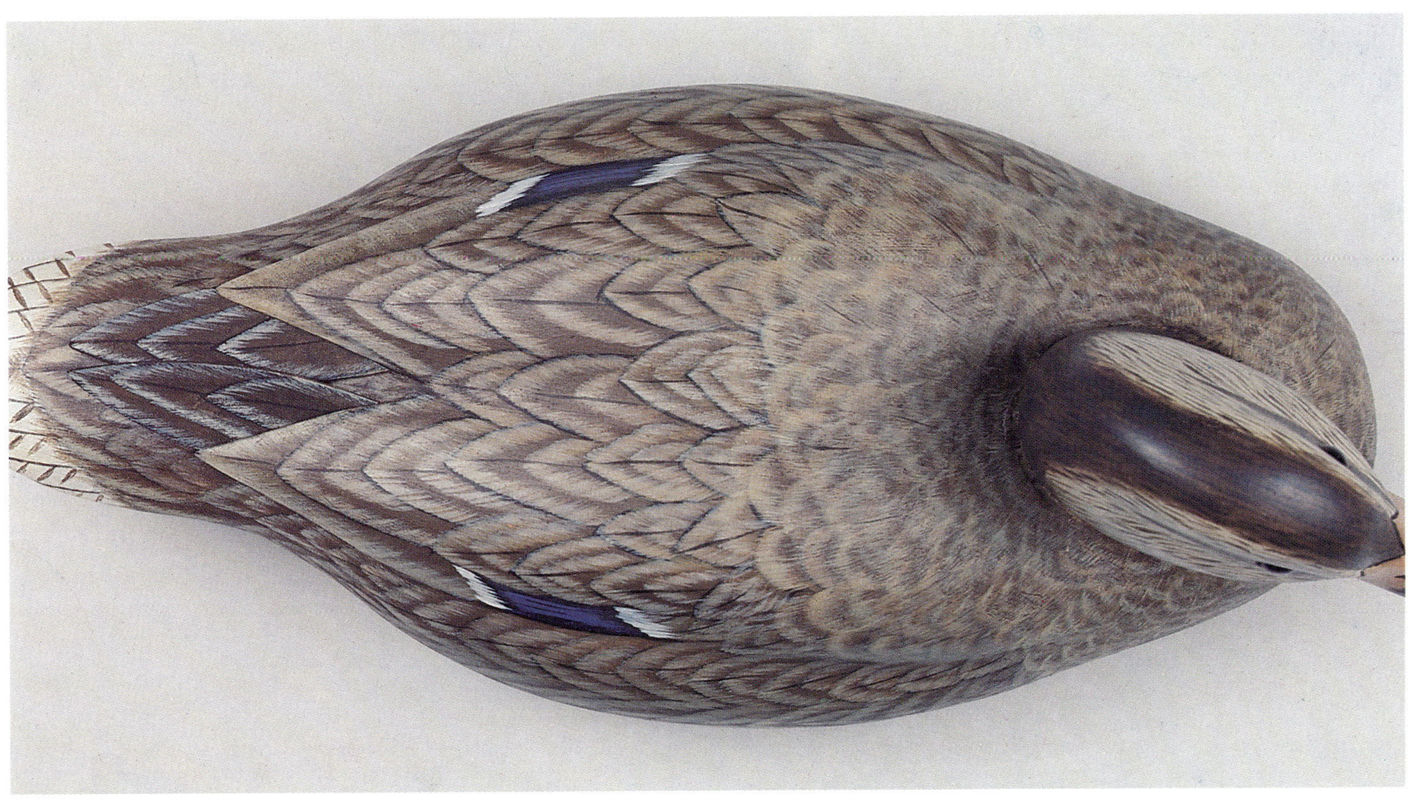

**Detail** - ***Back Area***
*The feather pattern on the back area of the Mallard Hen is painted in a defined manner. Note the linework that divides the feathers.*

# GREEN WINGED TEAL DRAKE

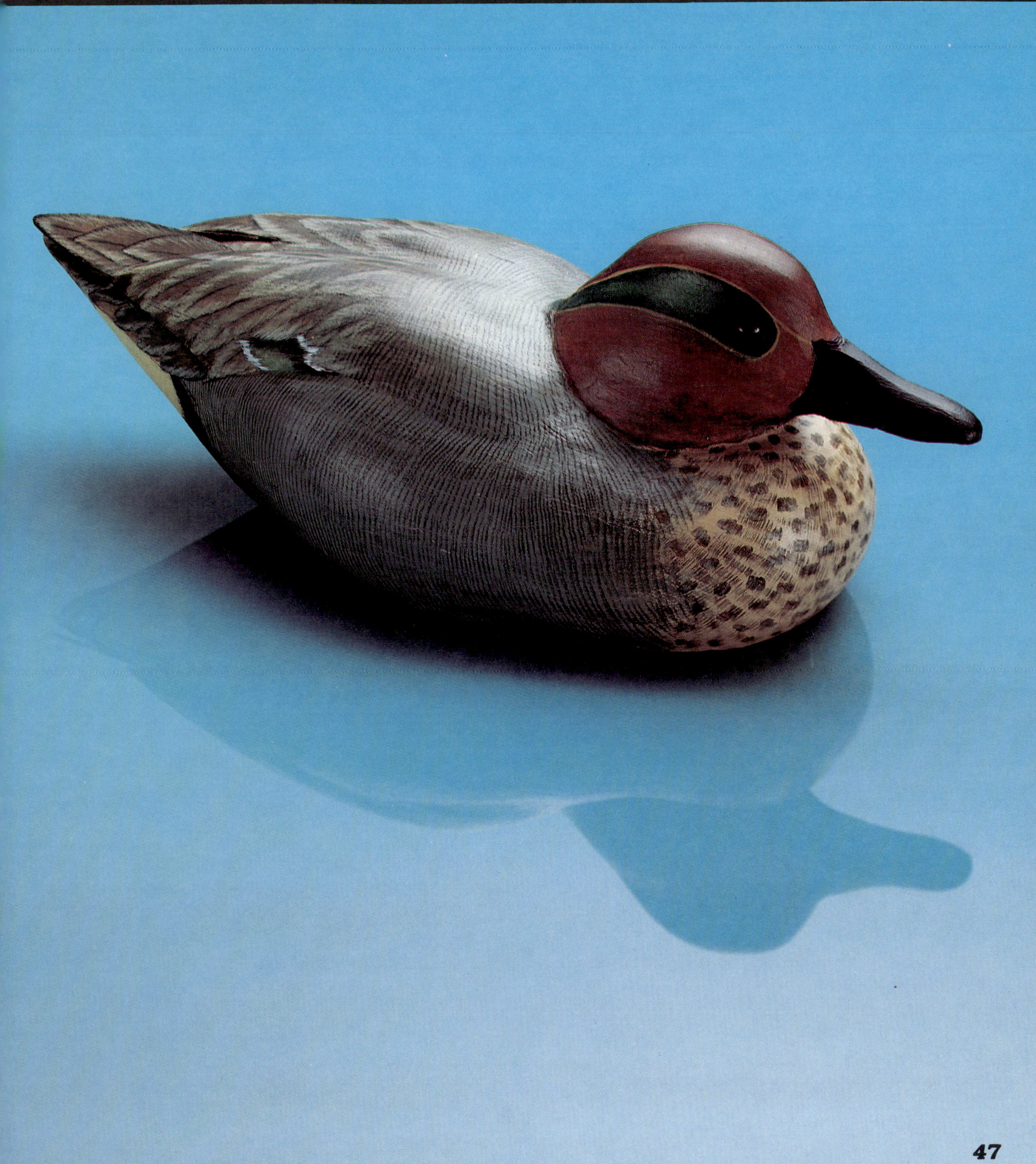

# GREEN WINGED TEAL DRAKE

**Permalba Colors**
White
Unbleached Titanium
Black
Raw Umber
Burnt Umber
Burnt Sienna
Phthalo Green
Yellow Ochre
Cadmium Yellow Medium
Iridescent Gold

**Brushes**
Beebe Hopper Liner #0
Beebe Hopper Shader #1
Beebe Hopper Shader #10
Beebe Hopper Shader #18
Beebe Hopper Kats Tongue #12

*Ivory Black + Unbleached Titanium = Color mixture*

***Illustration #45***
*Shown above are color chips for the mixture to be used to base the shoulders and sides of the Green Winged Teal Drake. Ivory Black is added to Unbleached Titanium to create a middle value gray for these areas.*

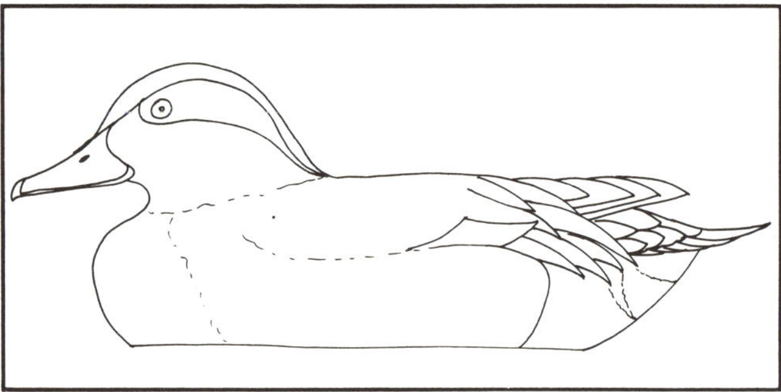

***Illustration #46***
*Feather placement diagram (Side view). Follow diagram for general placement of feather strokes on the wing and tail areas.*

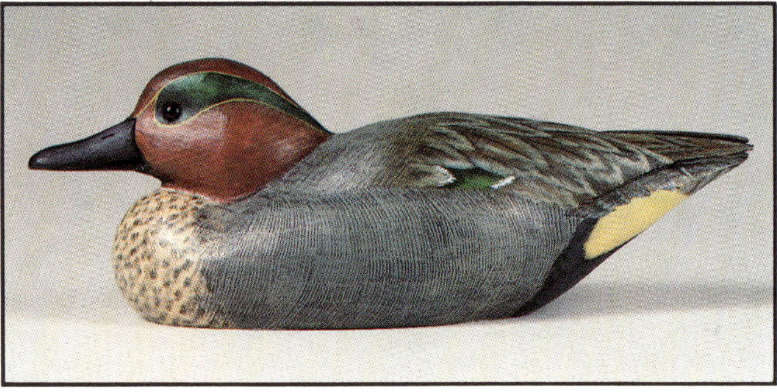

**Detail - *Side View***
*Note the feather placement and vermiculation technique on the side area of the Green Winged Teal Drake.*

Before beginning to paint the Green Winged Teal Drake, you should lightly sand the decoy to be sure it is smooth. Then apply a wood sealer to entire decoy and let dry. After the piece is sealed, apply a primer. Be sure primer is dry and lightly resand.

### Shoulders and Sides

Base coat the shoulder and side areas with a medium gray mixture of Ivory Black and Unbleached Titanium. Refer to color chips - Illustration #45. Create vermiculation over these areas in Ivory Black. Vermiculate using method of your choice. For this carving the brush method was used with the Beebe Hopper Shader brush #18. See section on vermiculation for further details. Refer to Illustration #46 for feather placement.

### Back

Base coat lower back with Raw Umber. Using a Liner brush and thin consistency Raw Umber, draw in the feather outline using feather placement diagram as a guide. Refer to Illustration #47. Shade inward from outer edge of each feather with Unbleached Titanium using Beebe Hopper Shader brush #10. Apply a wash of thin consistency Raw Umber on the Unbleached Titanium feather strokes. Refer to Illustration #47 for feather placement.

### Coverts

Apply Black with a touch of Iridescent Green added to the covert section. To softly blend, shade outer edge with Titanium White.

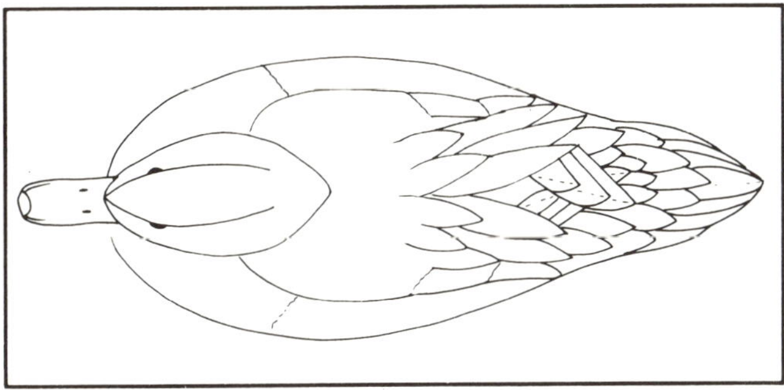

***Illustration #47***
*Feather placement diagram (Top view). To be used as a guideline for location of feather strokes on back and wing areas.*

*Burnt Sienna + Unbleached Titanium = Color mixture*

***Illustration #48***
*Shown above are color chips for the mixture used to base the breast area of the Green Winged Teal Drake. Burnt Sienna is mixed with Unbleached Titanium to achieve a mid-value warm tan tone.*

### Breast

Base the breast area in a mixture of Unbleached Titanium to which a small amount of Burnt Sienna has been added to achieve a pinkish tan hue. Refer to color chips - Illustration #48. Paint the markings on the breast area in Raw Umber and Ivory Black using the Beebe Hopper Shader brush #1.

### Head

Base the entire head shape with several coats of Burnt Sienna. Let dry. Then apply a thin consistency wash of Burnt Umber in crown area.

### Eye Patch

Base eye patch area in a mixture of Phthalo Green with a touch of Iridescent Gold added for highlight. Blend in a thin wash of Ivory Black around eye and at base of the crest. Outline edge in a mixture of Yellow Ochre and Cadmium Yellow Medium.

### Tail

Base the tail section in Raw Umber. Draw in feather outline with thin consistency Ivory Black. Shade inward from edge of feather with Unbleached Titanium using Beebe Hopper Shader brush #10.

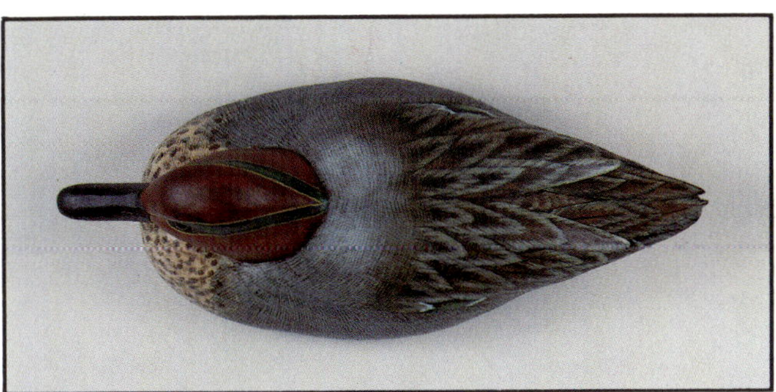

**Detail - *Top View***
*Refer to feather placement on the back area of the Green Winged Teal Drake.*

### Primaries

Apply a mixture of Raw Umber and a touch of Burnt Umber to the primaries. Draw in feather outlines using thin consistency Burnt Umber and a Liner brush. Shade from the edge of the feather inward with Unbleached Titanium. Apply a wash with thin consistency Raw Umber over the Unbleached Titanium feather strokes.

### Under Rump

Base the area under the rump with Ivory Black. To create the feather pattern, mix a touch of Unbleached Titanium with Black to make color a shade lighter than the base coat. Brush on feather pattern using Beebe Hopper Kats Tongue brush #12 fanned to desired size. Next, mix Yellow Ochre and Unbleached Titanium for the light patches of color on either side of the rump area.

### Speculum

Paint the central area of the speculum in Iridescent Green. Stroke on Ivory Black from the bottom area of the feather outward with a Liner brush. Next, stroke on thin, hair-like lines of Titanium White at both the tip and bottom edges of the coverts.

### Bill

Base the entire bill area in several coats of Ivory Black.

### Eye

If a dimensional eye is not used, coat the eye in Burnt Umber. Paint pupil in Ivory Black and highlight with Titanium White.

# GREEN WINGED TEAL DRAKE

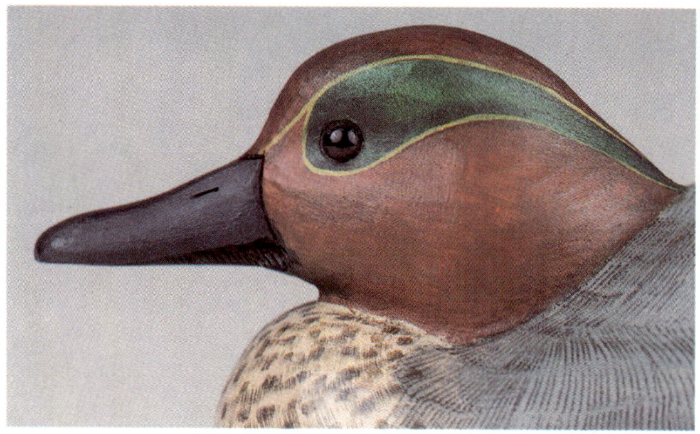

**Detail** - ***Head Area***
*The head area of the Green Winged Teal Drake is painted with unique markings. Note the green eye trough.*

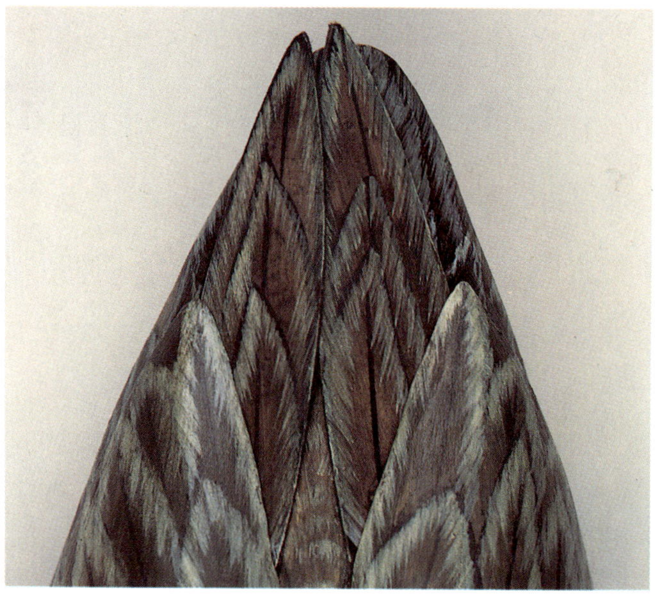

**Detail** - ***Tail Area***
*Take note of the stroke direction of the feathers in the tail area. These feathers are kept fairly light in value on the tips.*

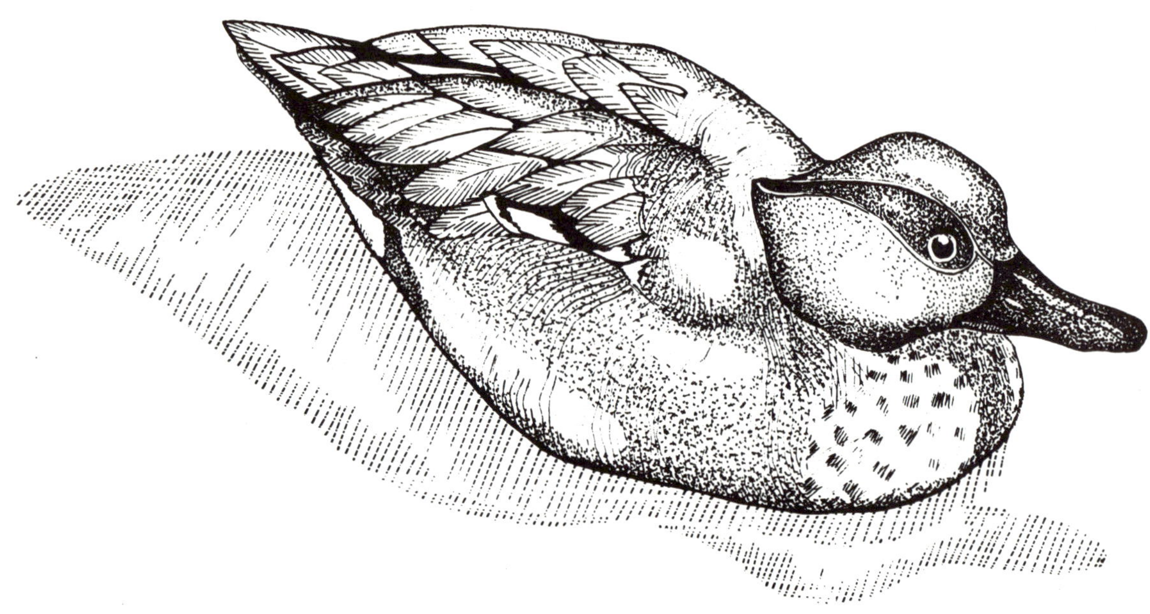

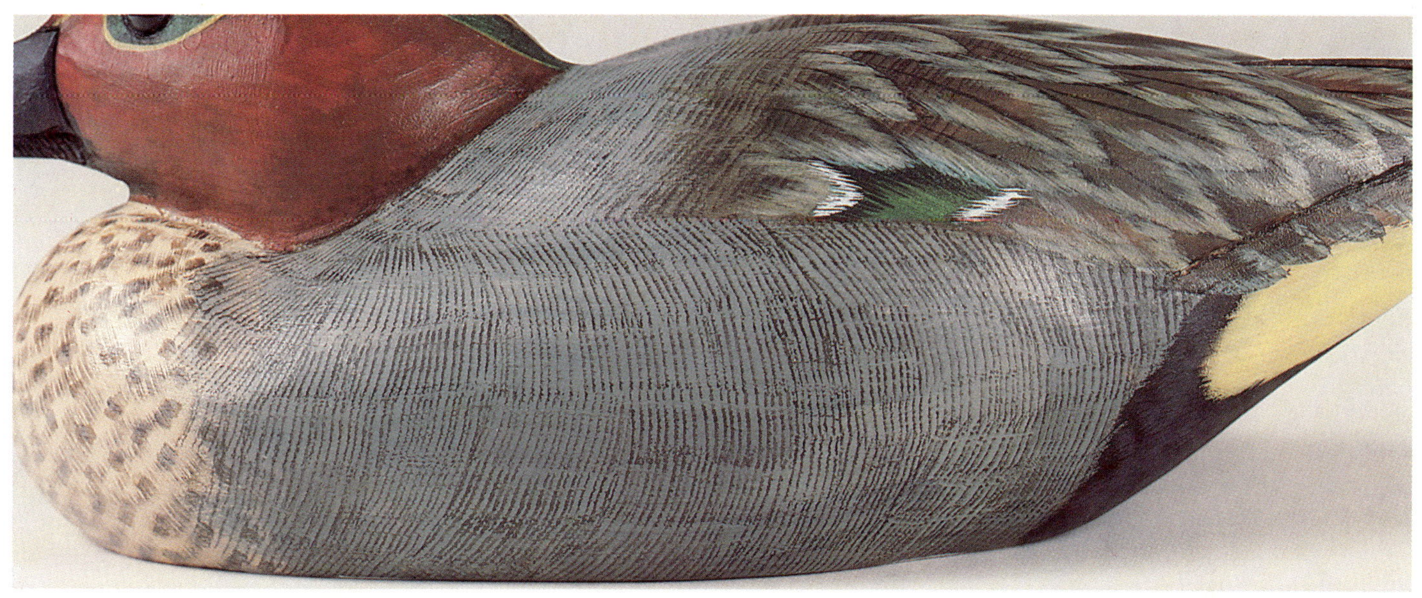

**Detail - *Side Area***
*Refer to this close-up photograph for stroking on feathers on the side area of the Green Winged Teal Drake. The feathers are created with the vermiculation technique.*

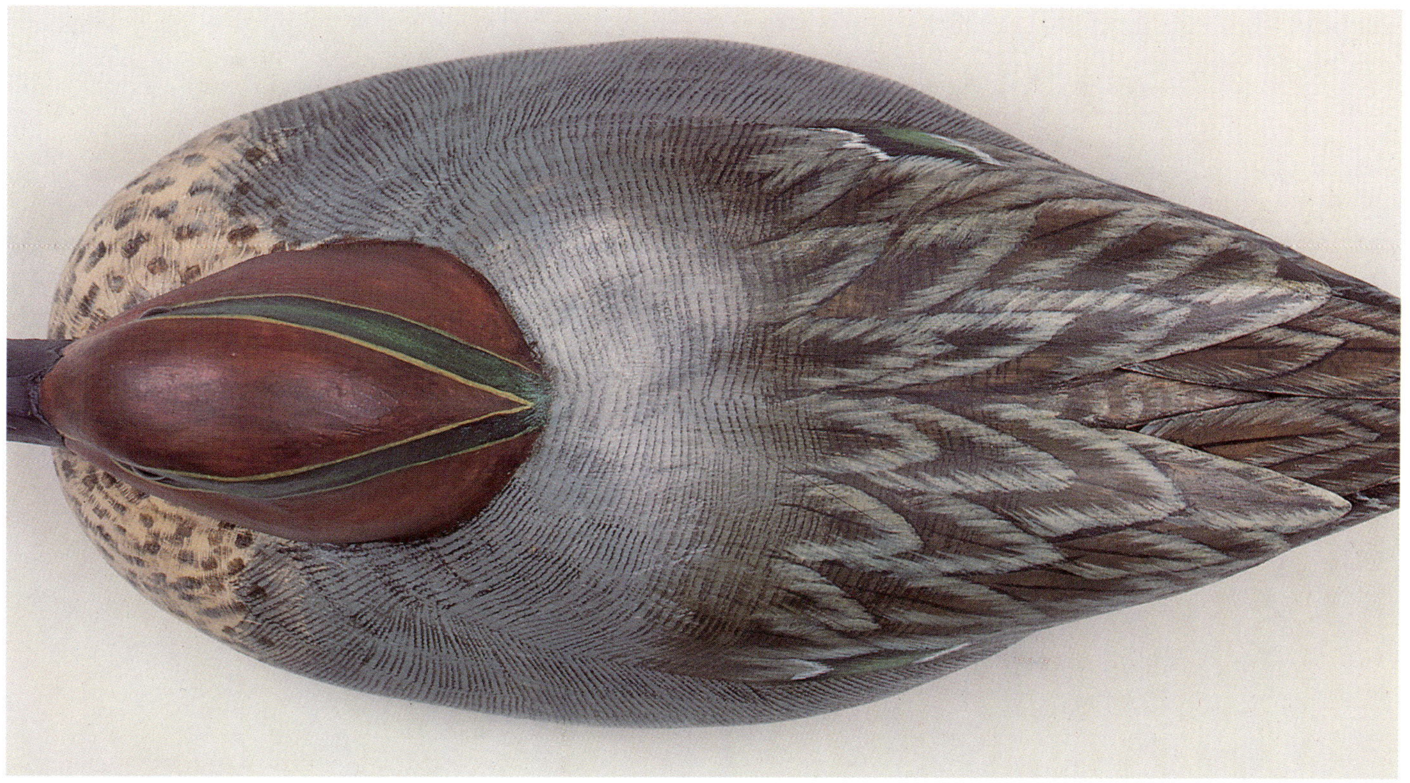

**Detail - *Back Area***
*The feather pattern on the back area of the Green Winged Teal Drake is created partially through the vermiculation technique and partially through feather strokes.*

# GREEN WINGED TEAL HEN

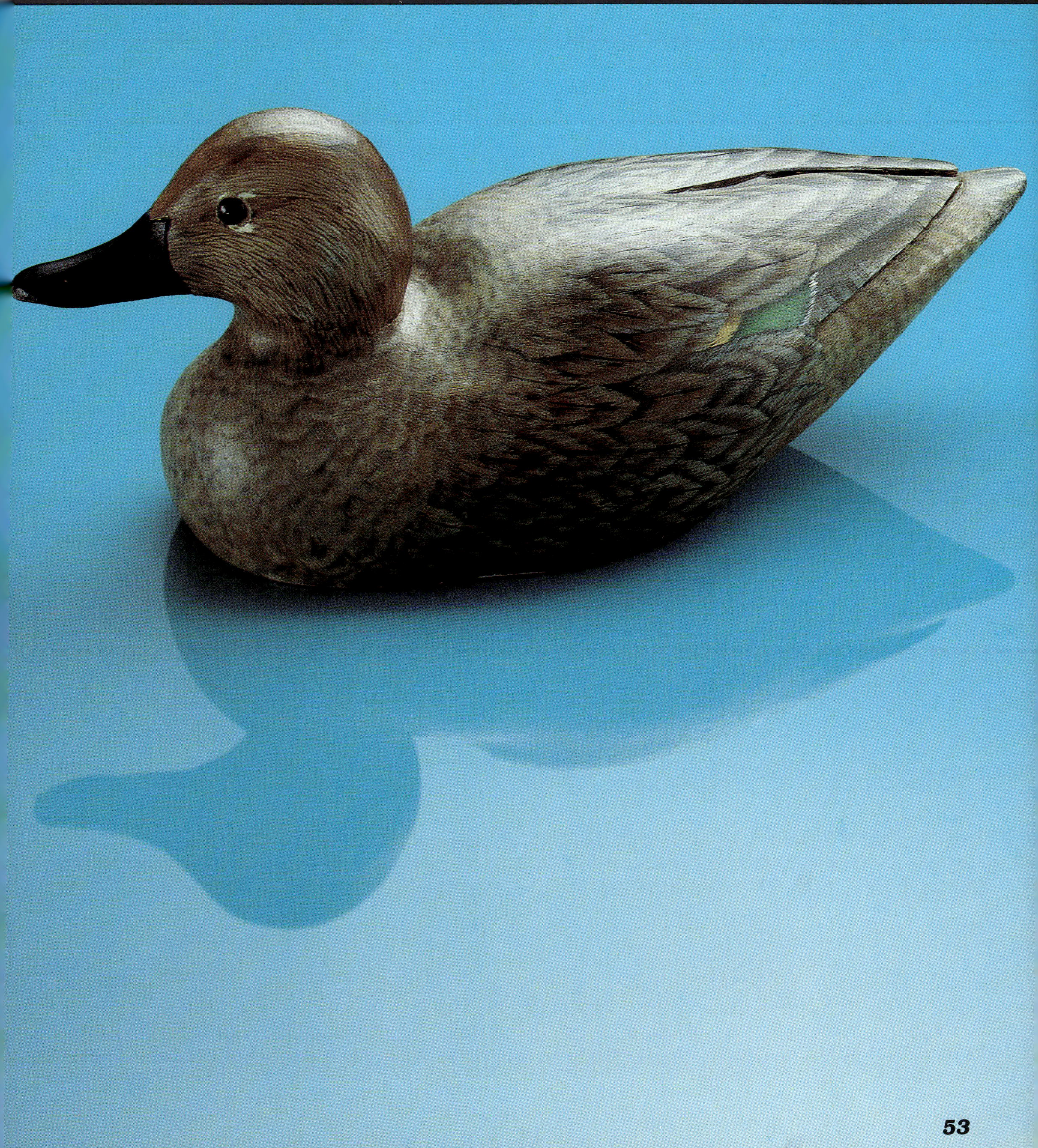

# GREEN WINGED TEAL HEN

**Permalba Colors**
Unbleached Titanium
Yellow Ochre
Raw Umber
Burnt Umber
Black
Phthalo Green
Cadmium Yellow Medium
Iridescent Green or Gold

**Brushes**
Beebe Hopper Liner #0
Beebe Hopper Shader #10
Beebe Hopper Kats Tongue #12

*Raw Umber + Burnt Umber + Unbleached Titanium = Color Mixture*

***Illustration #49***
*Shown above are color chips for the mixture to be used to base the body area of the Green Winged Teal Hen. Create the mixture by adding Raw Umber to Burnt Umber plus a touch of Unbleached Titanium = Color mixture*

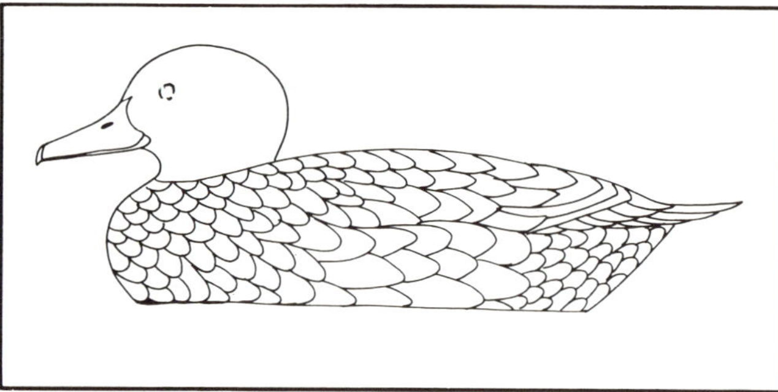

***Illustration #50***
*Feather placement diagram (Side view). Follow diagram for general placement of feather strokes on the sides, wing, and tail sections.*

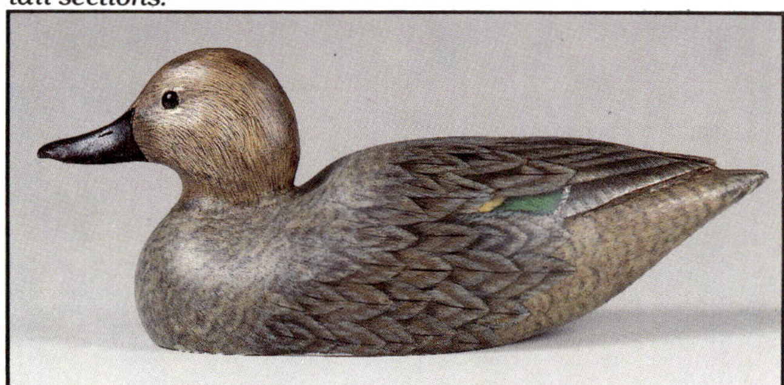

**Detail - *Side View***
*Note the feather placement and stroke direction on the side area of the Green Winged Teal Hen.*

Before beginning to paint the Green Winged Teal Hen, you should lightly sand the decoy to be sure it is smooth. Then apply a wood sealer to entire decoy and let dry. After the piece is sealed, apply a primer. Be sure primer is dry and lightly resand.

**Body**

Apply a mixture of one part Raw Umber, one part Burnt Umber with touch of Unbleached Titanium to the hen's body. Refer to color chips in Illustration #49.

**Back and Sides**

With thin Burnt Umber and the Beebe Hopper Liner brush #0, draw in feather pattern using feather placement guide. Refer to Illustrations #50 & #51. Create a mixture of one part Unbleached Titanium and one part Yellow Ochre to highlight the edges of elongated feathers using the Beebe Hopper Shader brush #10. The Green Winged Teal Hen feather has two highlighted areas, the second highlight area is half way down the feather. Repeat the same step paralleling the outer edge highlight. Refer to Illustration #52.

**Breast and Rump**

Using Beebe Hopper Kats Tongue brush #12 and Unbleached Titanium, make the feather pattern over breast and rump. After the feather pattern is painted over entire body, apply a wash with thin Burnt Umber. Then repeat feather pattern over entire bird and apply a

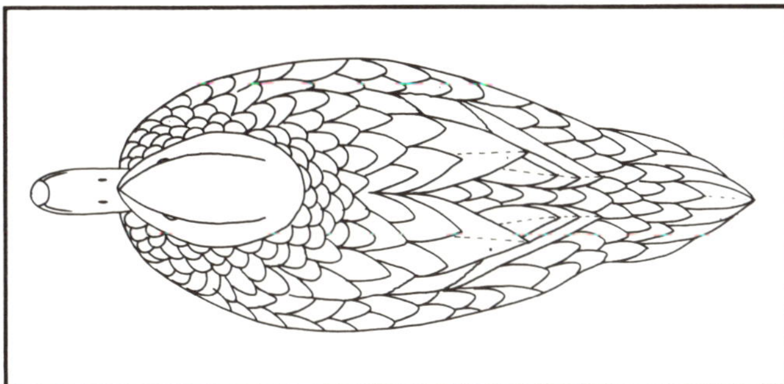

**Illustration #51**
*Feather placement diagram (Top view). To be used as a guideline for location of feather strokes on back and wing areas.*

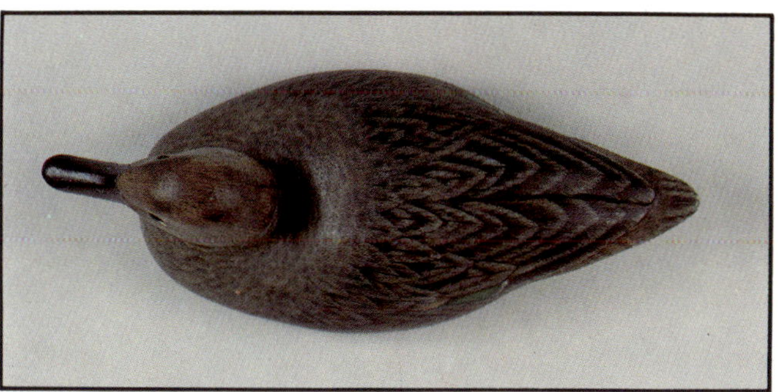

**Detail - *Top View***
*Refer to feather placement on the back area of the Green Winged Teal Hen.*

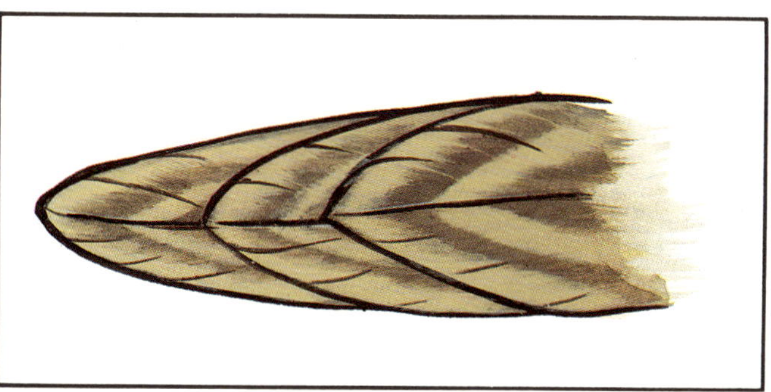

**Illustration #52**
*The main feather of the Green Winged Teal Hen has two highlight areas. One highlight area is at the tip of the feather, the other is at the half way point.*

*Raw Umber + Unbleached Titanium = Color mixture*

**Illustration #53**
*Shown above is the color chip for the mixture used to base the head of the Green Winged Teal Hen. Create the color mixture by adding a touch of Raw Umber to Unbleached Titanium.*

second wash with Burnt Umber. Continue this procedure of feather strokes and washes until desired softness is achieved.

### Head

Base the head in a light gray mixture of Unbleached Titanium and Raw Umber. Darken the crown of head and eye trough with thin washes of Unbleached Titanium and Raw Umber. Refer to color chip - Illustration #53 for color mixture. Darken the crown of head and eye trough with thin washes of Raw Umber and Burnt Umber. Blend mix up from neck and also down into body area to blend the head and body areas together.

### Primaries

Base the primaries in a mixture of Raw Umber with a touch of Unbleached Titanium. Draw in feather outline with thin consistency Raw Umber or Burnt Umber. Mix Yellow Ochre and Unbleached Titanium to apply feather strokes on edge of the primaries. Highlight from outer edge of the feathers inward with Unbleached Titanium using Beebe Hopper Shader brush #10.

### Tail

Apply Raw Umber to the tail section. Draw in feather outline with thin consistency Burnt Umber. Shade inward with Unbleached Titanium using Beebe Hopper Shader brush #10.

### Bill

Base bill in Ivory Black. Apply several coats.

# GREEN WINGED TEAL HEN

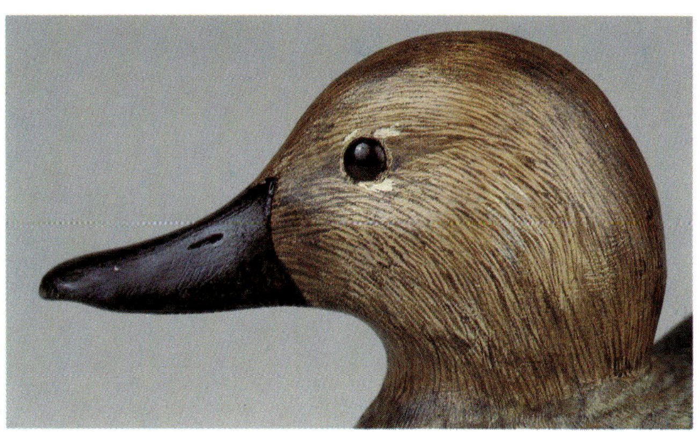

**Detail - *Head Area***
*The head area of the Green Winged Teal Hen has feather markings of dark linework. Note the slight darkness around the eye.*

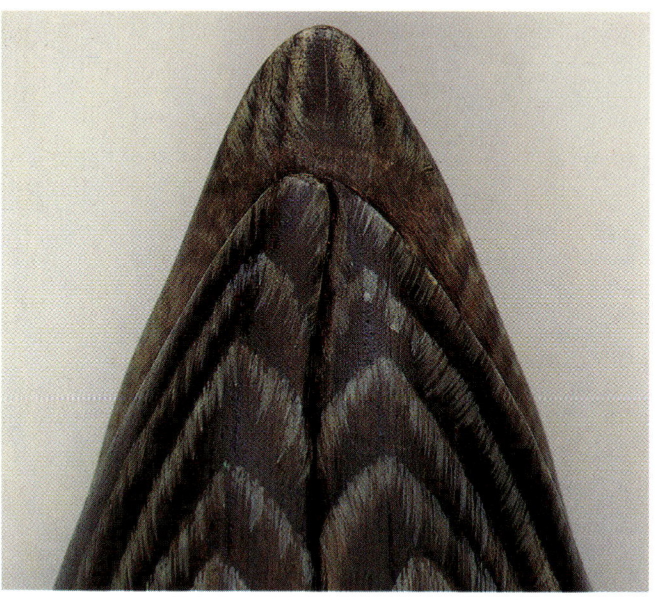

**Detail - *Tail Area***
*The small pointed tail area is painted dark in value. Contrast of light to dark is kept subtle through a series of washes.*

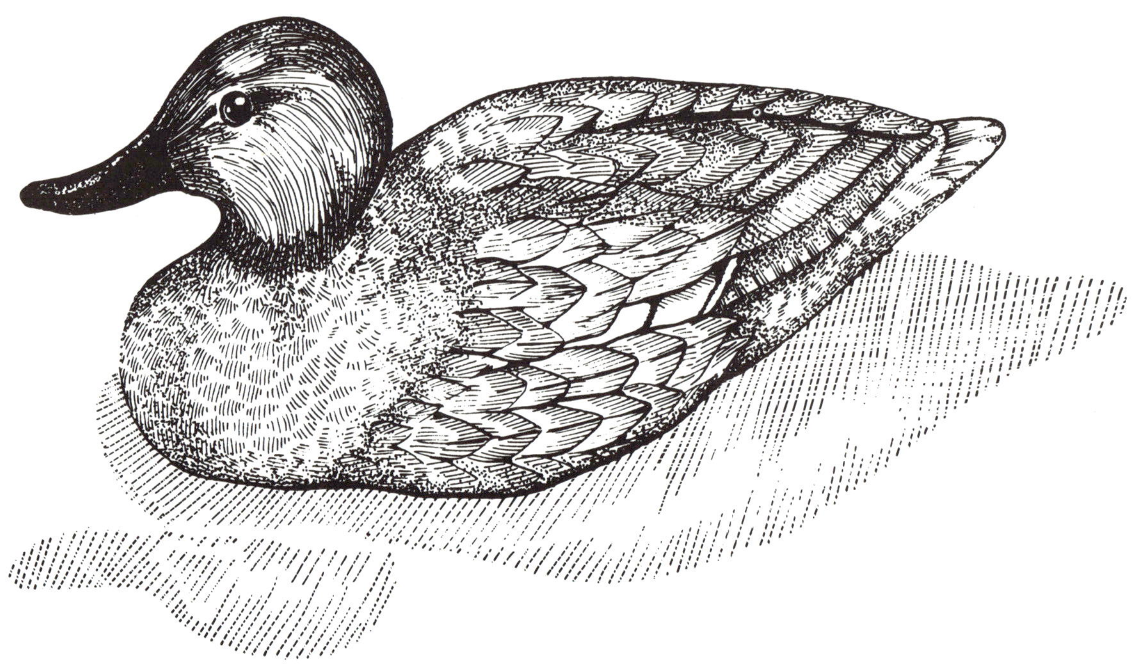

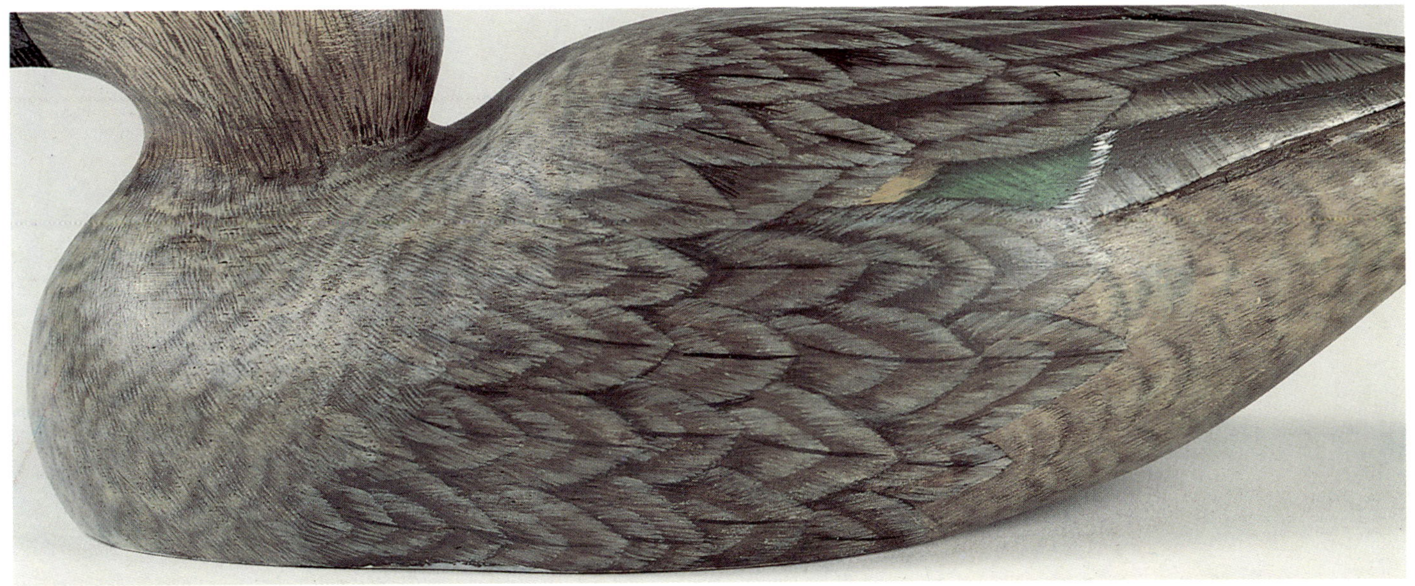

**Detail - *Side Area***
*Refer to this close-up photograph for stroking on feathers on the side area of the Green Winged Teal Hen. Note the distinct feather sections.*

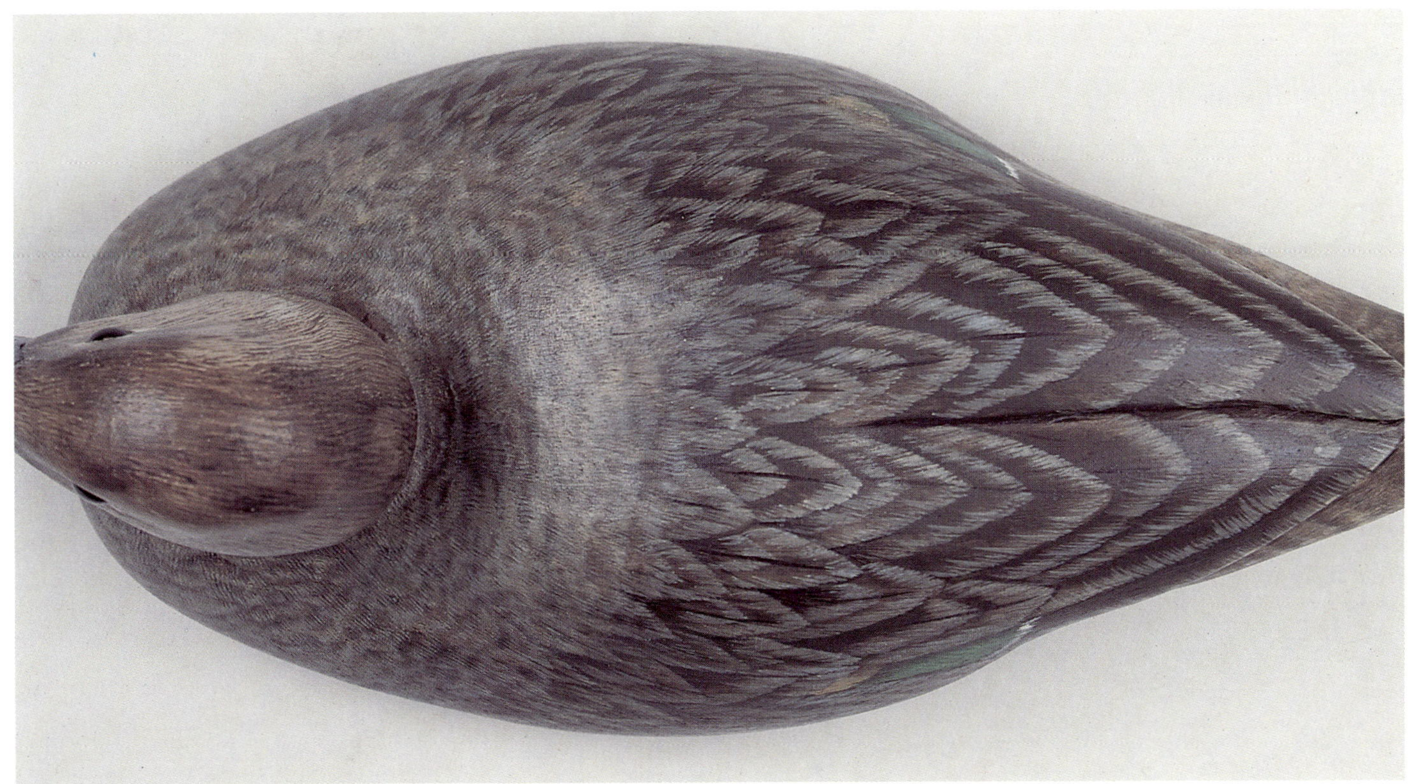

**Detail - *Back Area***
*The feather pattern on the back area of the Green Winged Teal Hen is created through distinct and separate feather pattern groups.*

# MALLARD MORNING

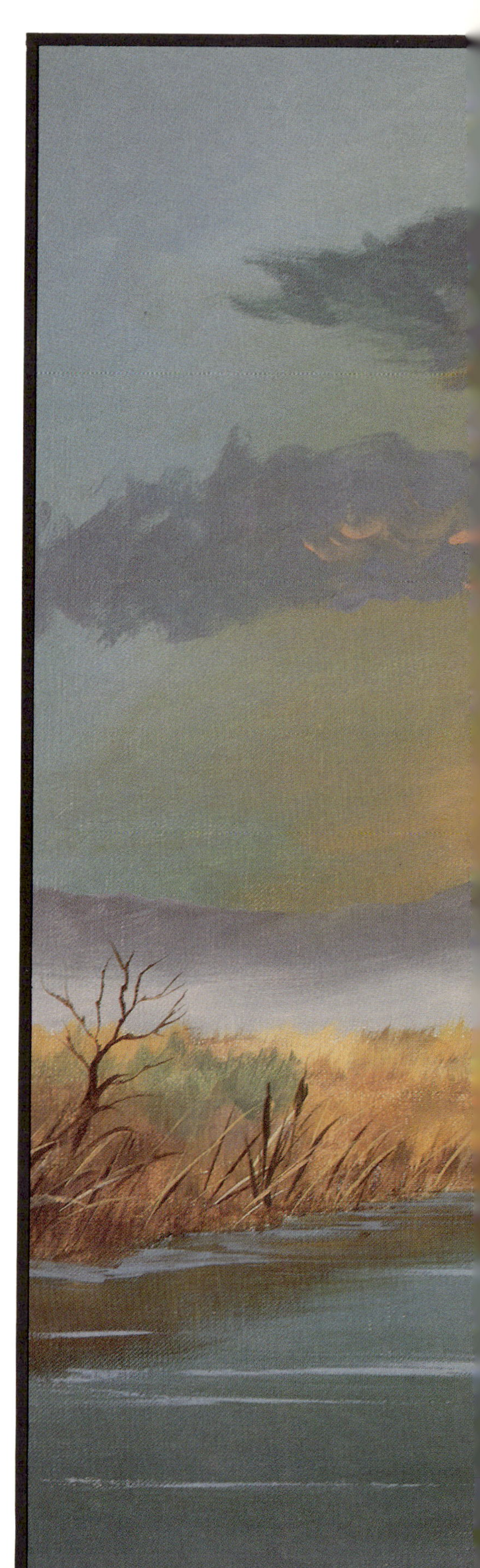

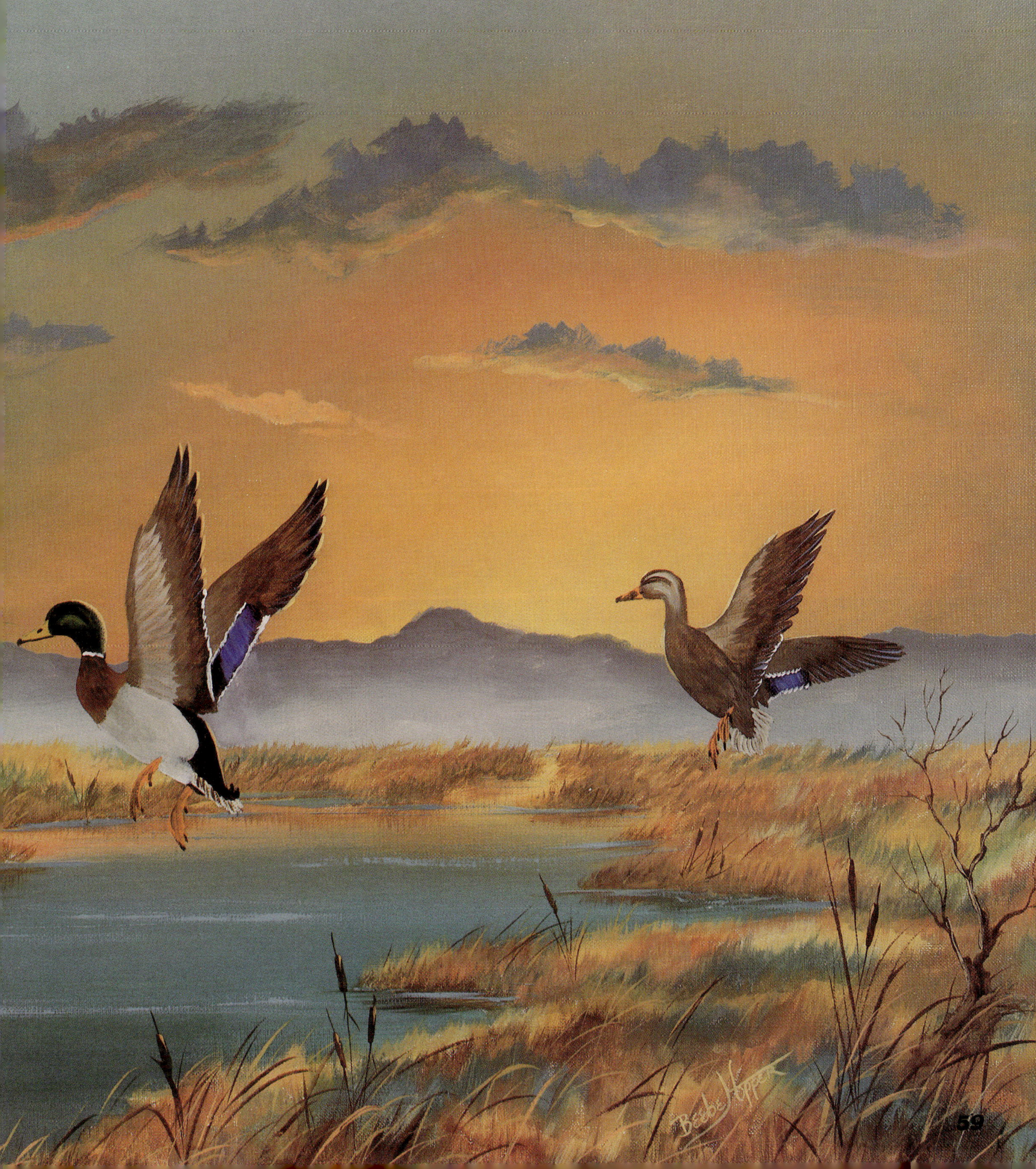
Beebe Hopper

# MALLARD MORNING

**Permalba Colors:**
Titanium White
Unbleached Titanium
Cadmium Yellow Medium
Cadmium Orange
Alizarin Crimson
Phthalo Green
Raw Sienna
Burnt Sienna
Burnt Umber
Hookers Green
Ultramarine Blue

**Brushes**
Beebe Hopper Liner #0
Beebe Hopper Shader #10
Beebe Hopper Shader #16
Beebe Hopper Shader #44
Beebe Hopper Kats Tongue #8
Beebe Hopper Kats Tongue #12
Beebe Hopper Kats Tongue #18

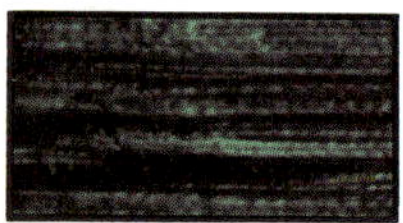

*Phthalo Green + Alizarin Crimson = Color mixture*

***Illustration #54***
*Shown here are color chips to create the mixture for the parent color used throughout the painting. Equal amounts of Phthalo Green and Alizarin Crimson are mixed together.*

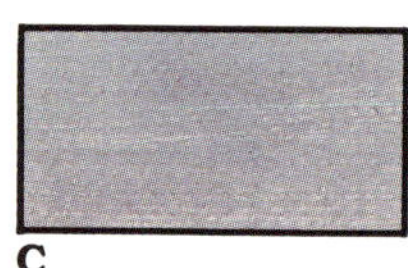

**A** **B** **C**

*A. Titanium White + Parent color + Phthalo Green.*
*B. Titanium White + Parent color*
*C. Titanium White + Parent color + Alizarin Crimson*

***Illustration #55***
*Shown here are color chips to create the mixture for the sky and water area.*

***Illustration #56***
*The sky area is shown here which is developed with a radius of the following colors softly blended together: Cadmium Yellow Medium, Cadmium Orange, Alizarin Crimson, sky blue mixtures.*

When painting on a canvas surface I use the finest portrait linen canvas, Fredrix Kent 125 DP. This type of canvas has a smooth surface and does not wear the hairs of your brushes as a coarse weave canvas would. For canvas painting, I use brushes with soft hairs to achieve smooth even blended tones.

Sketch the basic design onto the canvas with charcoal or a soft lead pencil. Paint the complete background which includes the sky, mountains and background marsh lands. When dry, superimpose the ducks onto the finished background. Transfer the images using tracing paper with graphite paper. This is an easy application method.

This painting is completed with acrylics, so you must keep in mind to work with a dampened canvas (surface moistened with water). This will enable you to blend your colors without the fast drying element of acrylics. Permalba Acrylic Retarder could be used, it prevents the paint from drying so quickly.

When painting a waterfowl scene, remember that a "marsh is a marsh" and the painting basics for a salt water marsh or a fresh water marsh are the same. The difference in these two marshes is the surrounding area; fresh water marshes have different trees, shrubs, foliage, etc. than the salt water marshes. It is advised to study the area you are painting.

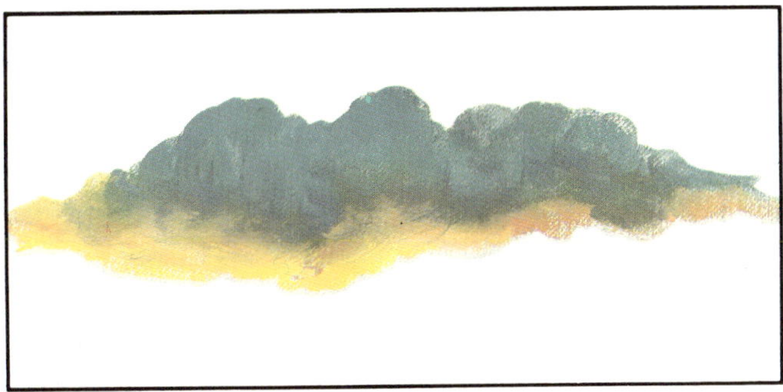

***Illustration #57***
*Deeper tones of the sky mixture are used to stroke in the cloud shapes. Cadmium Yellow Medium and Cadmium Orange are stroked on the bottom edges of the clouds as accents.*

***Illustration #58***
*The mountains are based in a violet-gray mixture. Create this mixture by adding more Alizarin Crimson to the sky mixture.*

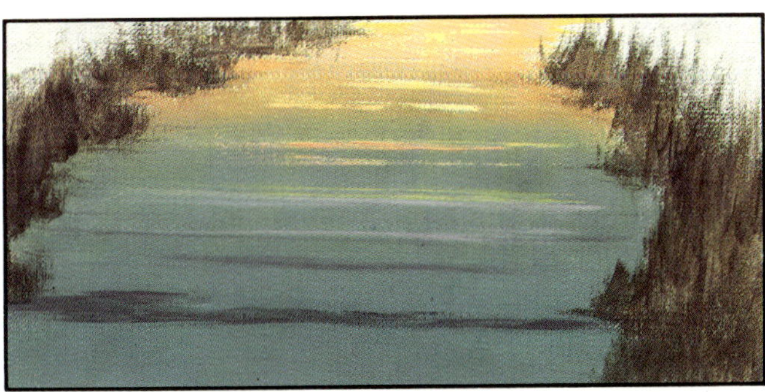

***Illustration #59***
*The water ripples are placed on the water area with the use of a palette knife. Place lines on horizontally to form water ripples.*

The first color that I mix for any painting, unless it is a monochromatic painting, is a very vibrant "black" made from one half Alizarin Crimson and one half Phthalo Green. Refer to color chips - Illustration #54. This is the parent color that I use throughout the entire painting. All the skies that I paint are made from this mix plus the addition of white. This color produces a lovely blue sky. For warmer tones in the sky area, add more Alizarin Crimson and for cooler tones, use more Phthalo Green. Refer to Illustration #55.

**Sky**

Using the Beebe Hopper Kats Tongue brush #18 or Beebe Hopper Shader brush #44, paint the sun area with Cadmium Yellow Medium and White. As you begin to brush outward from this area, add Cadmium Orange to the yellow mix and blend. Now, add a small amount of Alizarin Crimson to the orange mix and blend further outward. Gradually add the sky blue painted with the parent color as you move toward the outer edges of the canvas. Blend each color into the other. Remember to keep your canvas damp for easier blending. Refer to Illustration #56 for color placement and blending.

**Clouds**

Model the clouds using a Beebe Hopper Kats Tongue brush #8 with color variations of the sky tone mixtures. For strong contrast in the clouds, use deep tones to base the shapes in. Then stroke lighter tones into the area. Add accents of Cadmium Orange and Cadmium Yellow Medium to the bottom edge of the clouds. Refer to Illustration #57.

**Mountains**

Create a violet-gray mixture to base in the mountains by mixing the sky blue mix with a small amount of Alizarin Crimson. Using a Beebe Hopper Kats Tongue brush #12, paint the top edge of the mountain range. While this area is still wet blend Titanium White into the violet-gray mix toward the bottom area to give a foggy, misty, appearance. Refer to Illustration #58 for color placement.

**Water**

To paint the water area, begin at the horizon line and place the same warm colors as in the sky area. Begin with Cadmium Yellow Medium at the top area, adding Cadmium Orange and then add the sky blue mixtures. Darken the water slightly as you blend forward to the bottom of the canvas.

**Grass**

Using the Beebe Hopper Shader brush #44, in an upward flicking motion paint the grass area using these single colors plus brush mixtures: Burnt Sienna, Raw Sienna, Yellow Ochre, Unbleached Titanium, Cadmium Orange, Burnt Umber, and the sky blue mix. To achieve distance, the grass should be painted lighter and slightly grayed in color value at the horizon line.

**Water Ripples**

Using a palette knife angled on its edge loaded with the warm and cool sky colors, paint in the water ripples. Complete by drawing the knife horizontally to form line ripples on the water surface. Refer to Illustration #59 for details.

**Mallard Drake**

Block in the Mallard Drake using the following colors as guidelines. The mallard's head is based in Hookers Green. The bill is painted in Cadmium Yellow Medium. The mallard's feet are based in Cadmium Orange. The rump area is painted in the parent color mix used in the sky area. Wings of the mallard are stroked on in Raw Umber. The body is based in the light gray mixture used in the sky. The speculum is painted in Ultramarine Blue.

**Mallard Hen**

Block in the Mallard Hen using the following colors as guidelines. The mallard hen's body is based in varying tones of Raw Umber. The bill area is painted in Cadmium Orange and modeled with Mars Black. The hen's feet are painted in Cadmium Orange as well. The speculum area is painted in Ultramarine Blue.

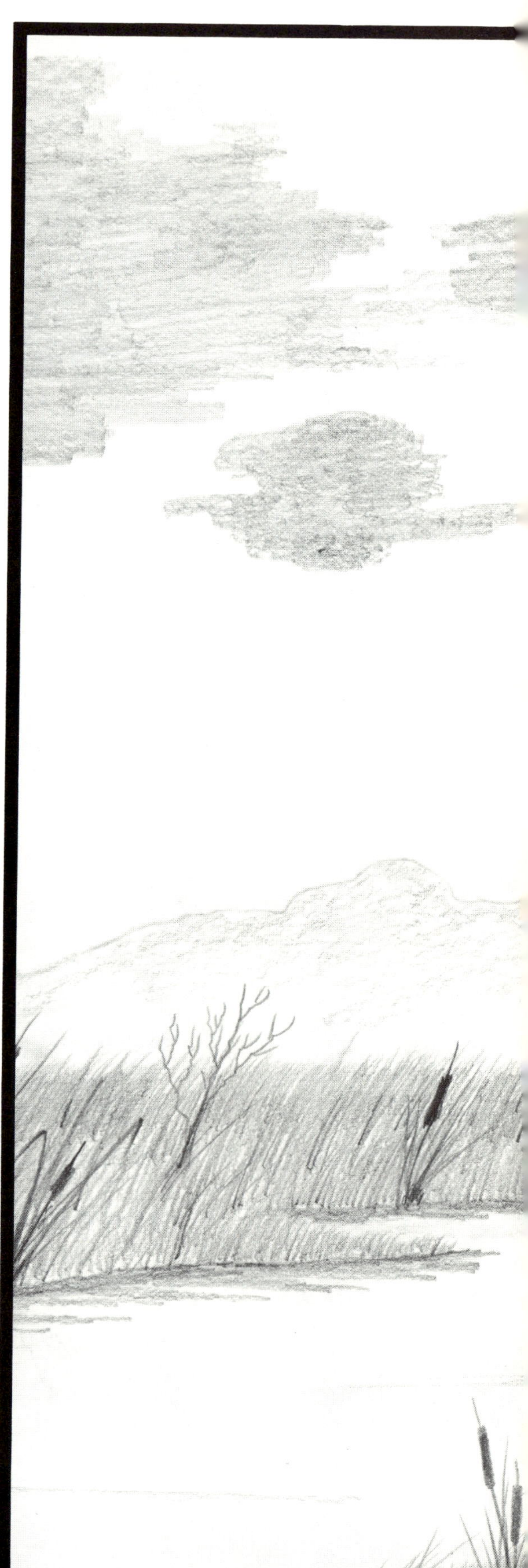

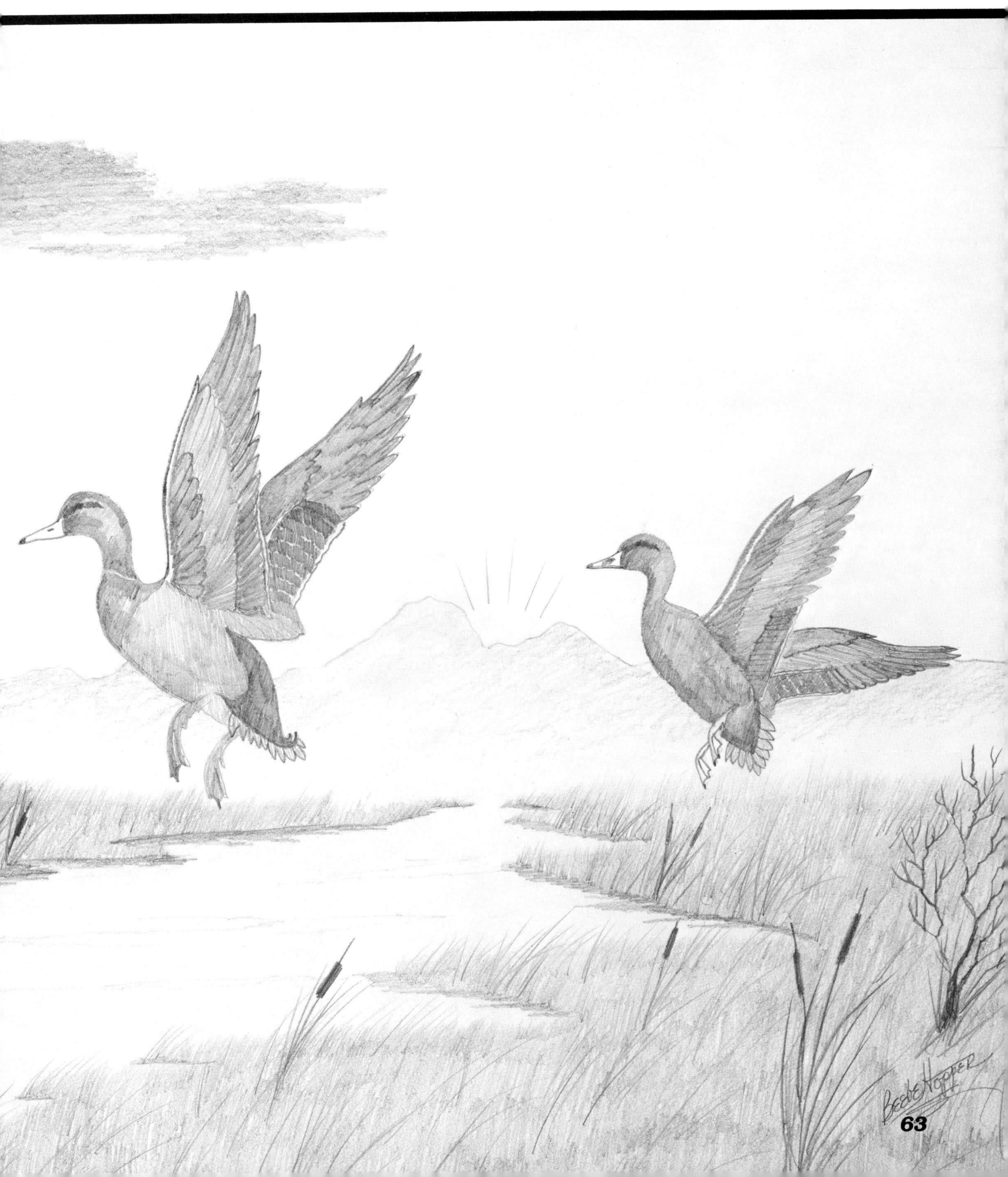
Beebe Hopper

## Additional Artwork

*Beebe Hopper is a versatile wildfowl artist. She enjoys working in a variety of mediums. Shown below are examples of her artwork completed in watercolor, etching, and oils.*

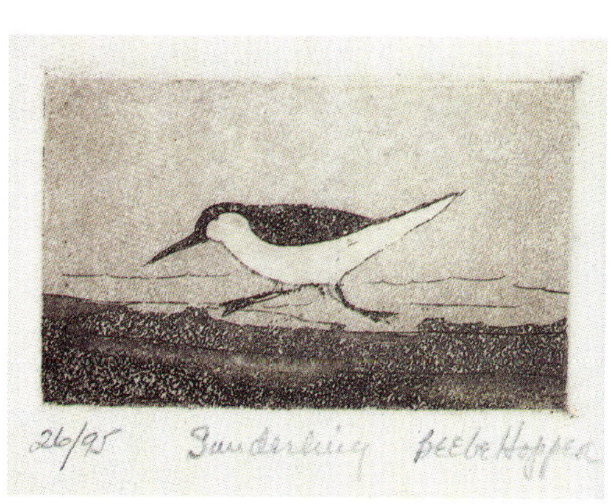


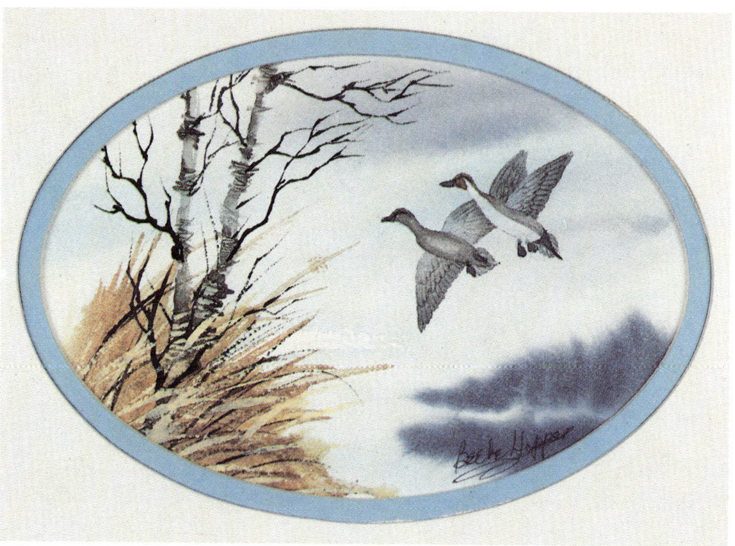


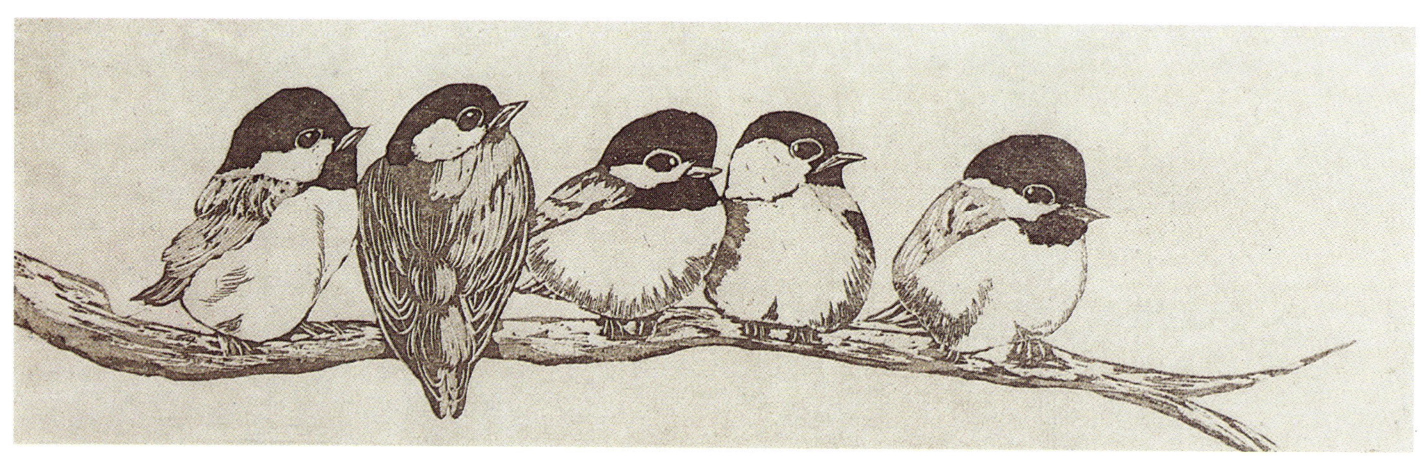

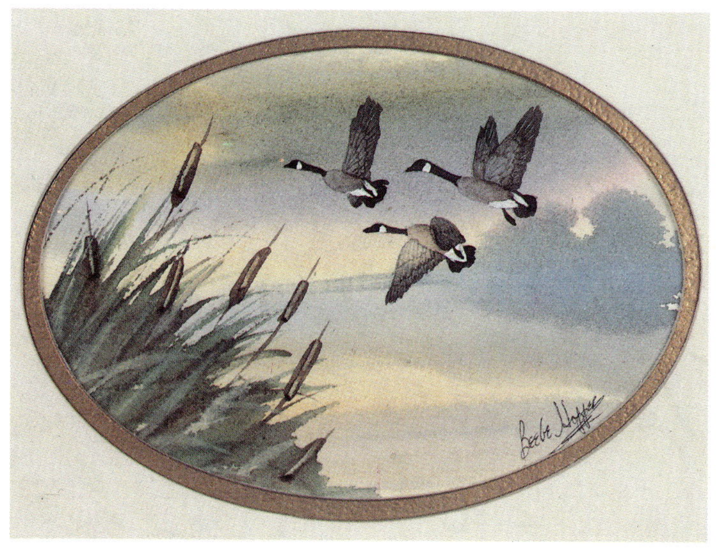


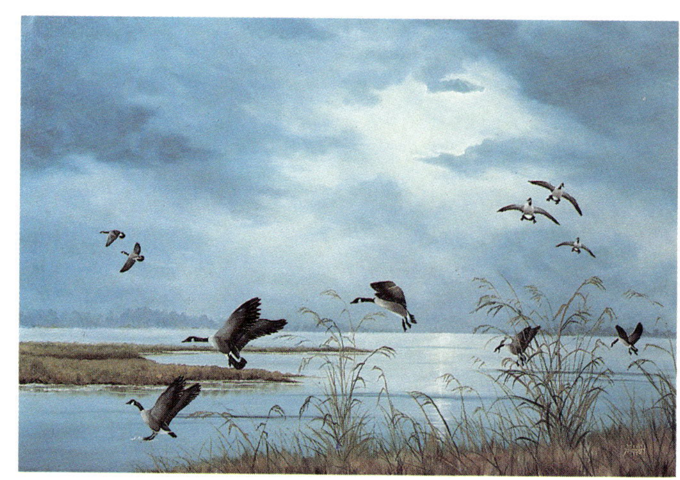